It Wasn't Funny at the Time

Stories from Maine Schools

It Wasn't Funny at the Time

Stories from Maine Schools

Terry Atwood

2019

First Printing: 2019
ISBN 978-1-79472-511-9

Terry D. Atwood
43 North Searsport
Prospect, Maine 04981
tatwood@fairpoint.net

Dedicated to my family who supported me over my 25-year career in public education. Thanks to my wife, parents, and children who put up with my long days, leaving before 6 in the morning, and often getting home at 9 after a school board meeting, game, parent meeting, or other evening event.

Special thanks go to my wife, Debora, for being a sympathetic ear when I needed to wind down after a stressful day.

And this book is for all the teachers I have worked with over the years, strong dedicated professionals who gave, and continue to give, their very best every day. They often take on the roles of mentor, unfailing supporter, and even become a mother or father figure for their students, providing stability when often school is the one stable place in that child's life.

Contents

Prologue
One Snowy Saturday
The First Day of School
Talk to the Parents, FIRST
Teacher Bloopers
She's a Good Teacher
The Screwdriver
The Escaping Breast
The Rats Leaving the Ship
Teenage Sexual Pranks
The Kindergarten "Accident"
Good Morning Meeting
The Wanderer
Snack Time
The Star Wars Light Saber
Beaten Up by a Five-Year-Old
The Curse
The Hallway Pass
Gross Events and Irrational Notes
The Ed Tech Sick Days
The Hot Fudge Sundae
Embarrassing the Boss
Don't Hit the Send Button
Out of the Mouths of Babes
Stupid Parent Tricks
Why is There an "M" in Our Name
"Pat" from Saturday Night Live
Would Not Have Happened
Free Turkey at Thanksgiving
The Trash Can
Don't Eat It

I Am Not Skipping School
The Doctor's Note
Teenage Raging Hormones
Outrageous Behavior
Teacher Stupid Tricks
The Knife Company

With gratitude I thank Diane O'Brien for helping me publish this book. As an author herself, she understood how much more there is to making a book than just the writing. I will be forever grateful for her kindness in taking on this project.

During my career working in public schools in the state of Maine I was astonished at the things that happened. Just when I thought I had seen everything, another unbelievable event would occur. So I decided to keep a journal, thinking that perhaps someday I would write a book. I kept adding to that journal over the rest of my career in two high schools, two elementary schools and one middle school. Now I've written that book, "It Wasn't Funny at the Time". In hindsight, a lot of it is amusing. You just can't make this stuff up.

Prologue

The son of a papermaker, I grew up in Bucksport, Maine, a mill town on the Penobscot River. The summer after high school graduation I got a job at St. Regis Paper Company working in the magazine room where workers dragged four-foot pulpwood logs with a pickpole out of the pile and into the grinder. Hard work, and sometimes in an eight hour shift we'd get only 15 minutes off. One night I noticed one old man (he might have been 40!) struggling to stand up after a break to get back to work, and it hit me: I'm going to make my living with my mind, not my back.

I joined the Air Force where I had a chance to literally see the world and get an education; over the next twenty years I completed undergrad and graduate school with a goal of going into education when I retired. I moved into administration after several years as a classroom teacher in various northern Maine schools, serving as principal and assistant principal at all three levels – elementary, middle, and high school.

As the top administrator in a high school, for example, the principal oversees the teaching staff, the curriculum, the custodial staff, food service, budget, transportation, and extra curricular/athletic events.

The assistant principal typically handles discipline issues. A parent may dispute a decision and take it to the principal, and if they're still unhappy, to the superintendent, and in rare cases, further to the school board. This last issue, student behavior, is where the unexpected can bring the whole tower of a day's duties tumbling down, or at least push it to the back burner.

One messy event might take up a whole day; scheduled teacher evaluations get cancelled, work on the budget put off, meetings at all levels re-scheduled, basically all other duties are put on hold. All so the principal can deal with an angry parent or student melt-down. The mountain of paperwork the principal is expected to handle every day, instead goes home with him to be completed evenings and week-ends.

One Snowy Saturday

It was a very snowy December Saturday. As I looked out the window from the comfort of my living room, right next to my wood stove, I thought to myself, "If this was a school day it most certainly would be a snow day cancellation. "I finished my first morning coffee and thought about going out to tackle some of this snow when the phone rang.

I looked at the caller ID – why was my superintendent calling on a Saturday morning?

"Terry. I need you to come in to my office right away."

"There's a blizzard going on; can't this wait till Monday?"

"No, it can't! I'm not asking, I'm telling you to come into the office."

"Can you tell me what this is about? I'll likely be two hours getting there."

"No I can't tell you on the phone, and I don't care how long it takes you to get here. You need to come in now." With that she hung up.

It was a long trip, 35 mph in driving snow, and me imagining all sorts of dire scenarios. The more I "spun" things in my mind the more anxious I became. After two and a quarter hours of white knuckle driving I arrived to find both the Superintendent and the Assistant Superintendent waiting for me. "Come on into my office and close the door," my boss said, "We'll be a while."

She started right in. "Terry, you have experience as a high school principal."

Of course, she knew that I did. I'd taken the job here as assistant principal just three months before, coming to this large high school from a much smaller rural high school where I'd been principal.

Then she came out with it. "You're now the principal here. Mr. J. has gone out on administrative leave." At my look of shock she added: "for personal reasons." Furthermore, since it was December, she went on, the likelihood of finding an experienced administrator to go into my position as assistant principal was unlikely. I would have to go it alone for the remainder of the school year.

I was the sole administrator in that high school for the remainder of the year, a tough year to say the least. From having to fire a teacher who was falling down drunk on the job, to suspending basketball players for threatening staff just prior to playoffs, to discovering drug dealing students, to high profile search and seizure cases, that first year as principal of a large high school was memorable.

The First Day of School

S he didn't sleep much that night in anticipation
of a day she'd dreamed about for literally dec-
ades, her first day as a classroom teacher. It had been a
long time coming. She'd finished college in May and in
September gave birth to the first of three children. Priori-
ties changed and the career she had longed for was
delayed well beyond what she had hoped.

Now though, it was her time. Who cares that she'd
be a first year teacher at 37? Her three children were in
middle school and high school, and she would finally
realize her dream, teaching in this northern Aroostook
County middle school in the great state of Maine.

She'd done her homework with lesson plans done
and folders to hand out. She'd even memorized the faces
and names of her seventh grade students through previous year photos.

School starts the first week of August in Aroostook
to allow for the three week "harvest recess" for potato
picking in late September and early October. Early
August in northern Maine is the most humid, sticky, uncomfortable part of a short summer, and her classroom
was on the second floor of a brick building with direct
sunlight. She'd brought in a large floor fan to keep the
room as comfortable as possible.

Everything was perfect. As the students began
arriving she greeted every single one at the door and
proudly called them by name. How impressive was that
to have your teacher know your name on day one?

The only downside so far was that it was higher
than 80% humidity and 80 degrees at 8 am. However,
she was determined to make all her plans for that first

day match what she had dreamed they would be. Students were all seated and she began taking roll call. She was just giddy with the thought that in a matter of minutes she would be molding young minds and helping them get an educational foundation needed to pursue their life dreams. Again, it was perfect!

Halfway through roll call she heard thunderous pounding on the floor. She looked up to see Johnny at a dead run for the front of the classroom.

"Johnny, what's the ...?" she started

"I don't feel very goo...." That was all he managed to get out before he vomited. Mind you, this was no ordinary vomit. This was vomit that had been churning with anxiousness about the first day of school. Couple that with sunshine baking through the windows on the second floor in a brick building with no air conditioning.

His forward momentum, along with his anxiety, added up to projectile vomiting. Think "The Exorcist". This ocean spray of vomit made a direct hit in the center of the fan that she had placed appropriately so that even students in the back would feel a little breeze. What they all got to feel was the warm, odor filled, green and brown vomit as it managed to hit every single one of them to some degree.

Now, in reaction, nearly a half dozen other kids began vomiting. Students got up and were running about the room in a futile attempt to escape the carnage. Some began falling as they ran on the slippery vomit-covered floor.

Ms. B realized this was bigger than she could deal with and she called the office secretary on the intercom. Both the principal and the secretary heard her panicked plea for help as well as students screaming in the background. Off he went on a dead run for the second floor, not knowing what he'd find.

Upon arriving and seeing the mess, he told them to line up and go to the nurse's office to clean up a bit, then go home and start school tomorrow. He told Ms. B to use her room phone to call each parent to come pick up their child, as a student had thrown up on them, and they were too soiled and upset to stay today. Once that was done she was to report to his office.

Ms. B spent the next two hours explaining to parents how their child had become a vomit magnet. She explained about the fan and her concern for the children's comfort in the heat. By this time, she was fighting off a growing urge to break into tears. This was supposed to be a perfect beginning to a perfect career that she had waited literally 15 years to begin.

She held it together long enough to see the last student safely into the care of a disgusted and put off parent who gave the teacher her first taste of a personal attack on her competency, complete with foul language. When she finally arrived at the Principal's office she couldn't handle it anymore.

Through whimpers and tears she explained to him her day, start to finish, how it had all played out, and what she had expected that first day would be like. She needed him to listen and he did. When she was finished and pretty much back under control, he replied with the one sentence that was not only dead on, but any educator can tell you sums things up perfectly: "Welcome to public education."

That principal was yours truly.

Talk to The Parents, FIRST

I suspended a high school girl who had told a teacher to do something that was clearly anatomically impossible. According to Mrs. G, an experienced, well respected, and award winning science teacher, she'd warned the student multiple times about her disruptive behavior during class. A poor student, the girl had already been suspended twice that year for marijuana possession and smoking on school grounds.

Mrs. G had asked her to come out in the hallway where, without an audience, she could ask the girl to "please, just let me do my job."

It is hard to talk rationally with irrational students. The conversation took a nose dive, and the girl became more disrespectful ending again with that particular profanity.

The teacher took the girl's elbow saying "come on, we're going to the office." The student, with more vulgarity, jerked her elbow away, smashing her own arm into the wall.

They both came to my office where Mrs. G told me what had happened. The girl validated the story, downplaying the original disruption, but not denying anything else.

After the teacher left, the girl and I had a conversation about how that could have been handled differently in an attempt to prevent any future occurrence. I spoke about how that level of disrespect and vulgar language at staff is not tolerated, and that, according to the student handbook, an automatic three-day suspension was called for. Since this was the last class of the day I had her sit in the office for the rest of the period, starting the suspension the next day.

Admittedly, I was not looking forward to speaking with her parents, people whom I had dealt with before and were difficult to say the least. I did ask some kids in the class about the incident and checked with the entire staff to see if any of them had witnessed it.

Not 30 minutes after the bus had left, the parents marched into my office, swearing all the way, yelling obscene adjectives about my competence.

"Look you asshole, you aren't suspending my kid for something that goddamn teacher did. Get her in here, I want her fired."

When I asked them to calm down they responded with the same suggestion their daughter had given Mrs. G. I told them if they couldn't calm down and talk rationally with me they would have to leave.

"Besides," I said, "am I yelling and swearing at you?" When they admitted I wasn't I replied, "Then why are you doing it to me?"

That had an immediate calming effect. To avoid an audience I closed my office door and said "Let me tell you what happened."

"We know what happened," said the dad. Their daughter had told them that after ONE smart mouth remark the teacher took her out in the hall and threw her up against the wall.

There it is, lesson number one from this incident. ALWAYS tell parents BEFORE the student gets home what happened so they have at least an opportunity to hear the truth before their child paints a different picture, that once told, is gospel.

I spent what seemed like an eternity getting them back to a point where they would even listen, and they never did believe the truth. They'd already spoken with other students, who had heard the thud of the girl's arm hit the wall when she jerked away. None of them had actually seen the incident.

I was firm in saying I'd investigated and could only substantiate what the teacher had told me. Now they were angry again, saying I was protecting the @#%$@# teacher. I insisted that the suspension stood.

At this point the dad threw his jacket down, put up his fists, and said "Let's go, right now."

"Please leave or I'll call the police."

When he lunged at me, the mom pulled him back saying "Screw him, we'll go see his boss."

The next morning I got a call from the superintendent who said she had supported me, but wanted the details. She told me the parents said I was swearing at them. Apparently when I said "I can't substantiate that" they thought I was swearing.

From that point forward for the rest of my career in public education, I made sure I knew the background, socio-economic standing, and as much as I could about parents. I made darn sure I spoke with words they understood. This is just ONE example of how experience served me great lessons that I didn't get in graduate school.

Teacher Bloopers

One distinct advantage of written communication is generally you can read what you write before hitting the "send" button. You edit mistakes, fix grammar and spelling errors and analyze what you've written for accuracy. Verbal communication has advantages like watching the body language of the receiver and adjusting your message accordingly to be less hard hitting or more direct.

But with verbal communication there's no "delete" key. Once you've said it, you've said it. You can correct what you've said, but that does not change the fact that you said what you said. It's like shutting the barn door after the horse got out. The cause is fixed but you cannot recover from letting out the horse.

Teachers are professionals, but they're also human. When they mess up verbally, it haunts them for a long period of time. With a teenager's raging hormones, high schoolers pounce on slip-ups, giving almost anything a sexual connotation.

Ms. T, a young and newly-married English teacher, was a perfectionist. She rarely made mistakes and when she did she generally was able to recover nicely. However, this one word slip haunted her for as long as she remained at the school. The legacy got passed from class to class and teens relished in sharing it with classes that were to come.

Ms. T was introducing a book they were going to read; "Ok, we are going to start off this quarter reading a great book called the 'Tale of Two Titties'".

At first, she was completely perplexed at the uproar of laughter. She truthfully had no idea what she had said until a girl in the front row explained. Future classes took great delight in asking her what book they were going to read when they got to that unit, invariably with an impish grin on their faces. It took just a second to reap years of embarrassment.

I was the assistant principal at a high school when my boss, the principal, announced at an assembly that "Mr. Atwood wants to now tell you about his nuts and bolts." The general information I was going to share with the student body was lost.

That same principal, explaining the importance of interviewing and public speaking skills, said to a class of high school students, "Sooner or later you'll all have to sell yourselves to someone."

A home economics teacher told a group of boys in her cooking class, "Ok boys, it's time to chop up your nuts."

Ms. D, the guidance counselor, told a class of boys signing up for classes, "I'll service all the freshman boys."

Mrs. M was an outstanding school secretary, well organized, able to handle anything, good at crossing the "t"s and dotting the "i"s. I was the assistant principal in that school with discipline my main duty. It was back in the day of paper records; we used a triplicate form, sending one copy to the teacher involved, one to the parents and one remained on file.

Mrs. M had heard me complaining about the form, an odd size, not working well in regular hanging folders, and she seemed genuinely pleased when she entered my office one day and announced she had a solution. "Jane Doe has got a REALLY nice box and I think you ought to take a look at it."

All I did was smile. That's it – smile! Is there any harm in that?

Mrs. M would jot things down and put the notes in my box for me to handle when I got to it. Sometimes it felt like I was doing triage. One particularly volatile day students waiting to see me for discipline issues – swearing, disrespect, disruption, etc. – were stacked up like cord wood in the office. I hadn't had lunch at all and it was 1:30 or so when Mrs. M handed me this note: "Joe was sent out of class for being nude and not cooperating." I burst right out loud laughing as all I could do was picture this kid brazenly giving that teacher a hard time in the buff.

During a long string of placement meetings, held to determine the make up of the next year's classes, we all cracked up at a note from a teacher that read: "I feel very strongly about this and I am happy to come see this committee and explain why if you want me to do so, but I really believe Johnny needs to be placed in Mrs. Smith's ass. Her ass would be the best fit for Johnny." It was a fitting end to a trying and what had been a somewhat contentious meeting.

Ms. W, a caring teacher, used a Jeopardy-like game to review material before testing. She gave prizes, practical things that she knew her students could use given the homes most came from – a new towel, perhaps a pair of jeans, sneakers, etc. She spent money at yard sales and Goodwill for her "stash." She always laundered all the clothing before it went into the prize box.

But one time she had washed some of her own clothing with the prizes. In a hurried rush to fold, store, and get them to school, she inadvertently took something of hers inside the folded clothes, and it all went into the prize box. She wanted to crawl in a hole when a sixth grade boy pulled a pair of the teacher's panties out of the prize box. Ms.W gave me a heads up about it as quickly as possible so that I would able to address any parent calling. She didn't find my giggling to be humorous whatsoever.

One time Ms. C, the speech and language specialist, came strolling into an Individualized Education Plan (IEP) meeting 10 minutes late. As she took her seat, the parent at the meeting, who had wanted to know why she wasn't there, gave some body language indicating she was displeased with the tardiness. Ms. C said, "Sorry I'm late getting here. I got stuck in traffic behind someone who obeys traffic speed laws." This brought a chuckle from all, and the meeting went off without a hitch.

Mr. J, the U.S. history teacher, was passionate about history; enthusiasm came shining through in every lesson he taught. Students gravitate to such passion, and it can become a catalyst for learning.

One day he was talking about how much of the world disliked the Brits when they seemed to be colonizing the world. He feverishly explained how the British kingdom-building wasn't palatable to many countries, and how those countries supported resistance to the Brits. People in the U.S. were becoming more and more resistant to British rule, he said, and even "the French supported an insurrection in the Mississippi delta."

Actually, that was what he meant to say. What he actually said was, "the French supported an erection in the Mississippi Delta." For a fraction of a second, students were dumbfounded by this, looking at each other as if to confirm they had heard what they just heard. By this point, the teacher was well beyond this and further into passionately making his point about the view of British world colonization.

That's likely why about three seconds later, he was taken aback by the laughter that rocked the room. The next door teacher came over to be sure everything was alright. Mr. J bellowed "Quiet!", absolutely clueless as to what precipitated this behavior. Certain types of laughter cannot be harnessed and held back if one finds something so funny that they literally can't help it. This was one of those times.

Mr. J was also known as someone who NEVER sent students to the office, priding himself on outstanding classroom management. He demanded loudly to be told what was so funny. Finally one brave young woman told him what he said. I was told by some very reliable students that the look of utter shock and dismay on his face, was a moment in time that NOBODY in that class will ever forget. At that class's 20th reunion it was undoubtedly discussed, relived, and more laughter had by all.

However, I will end this story by saying these students have a strong sense of U.S. history, and learned a great deal from Mr. J, a teacher who never gave less than 100% on whatever he did.

Ms. R stopped me in the hall one lunch hour to explain that her intercom wasn't working. I'd been trying to reach her all morning.

"Mr. Atwood, I didn't do what you asked because my ding-dong isn't working. Does your ding-dong work?" Students walking by were trying their level best to fight back laughter. This teacher didn't have a clue. I don't think this story needs further explanation.

During the four- minute transition time between classes, with the halls full of students, the guidance counselor called a teacher via the school wide intercom. She knew the teacher was expecting something in the mail and she'd noticed that it had come in. "Mr. Smith" she said, "please come to the office. You left your big package here. Mr. Smith, please come get your big package." Again, if you've ever dealt with teens you can figure out what happened from there.

One ed tech (educational technician) was a bit scatter brained. She deeply cared about kids and did a great job, but did and said things without a clue of the implications. One time she happened to be in the outer office talking with the two office secretaries while I was sitting in my adjacent office; sound carried very well through the door, and I could hear even very low conversations.

The UPS man was walking up to our building, struggling with an armful of packages. As he came through the door, holding it open with his foot, a couple of the packages fell off the top off the pile he was carrying. The ed tech was facing the counter with a view of this whole thing. The secretaries were facing away and didn't see it happen. I don't know why the woman chose these words but I can tell you the result.

"Oh look", said the ed tech with a view of the door, " the poor man was only half way in and he lost his load." Bear in mind, I could hear what was said, but had no view. Of course, hearing that phrase, I had to go check out what the heck she was talking about, particularly when both secretaries were trying their level best to contain themselves, but beginning to fail.

The ed tech left the office without a clue. As soon as she was gone both secretaries lost it. They had tears rolling down their faces from laughing so hard. I felt bad for the poor UPS man who was trying to figure out what was so funny. For the rest of the day, every once in a while, I would hear one of the secretaries giggling. That would get the other one going, and it went on for hours.

Then there was the business teacher who was showing students in an after school activity how to pan cook something. "If you do this right," he said, "it won't stick to your bottom."

I had a staff member who left his room with no supervision at the high school level without asking someone to cover for a couple minutes so that he could go use the bathroom. He left his laptop open with his password right next to his machine.

Ms. H taught math to high school juniors. She should have realized how they'd take her comment on that night's homework assignment: "Don't do 69, you won't like it or enjoy it because you won't know how to do it."

A teacher on lunch duty scolded a high school boy: "Somebody must pay for your dental work so stop chewing on that plastic fork."

"No they don't", the boy responded, "my parents are both dentists. "

She's a Good Teacher

Six-year-old Henry already had the reputation of being the first grade's Class Clown and Antics King, and it was only October. I was sitting quietly, and I thought unobtrusively, at the rear of the room observing his teacher, writing up the formal evaluation I did on every staff member. Henry was sitting directly in front of me.

Because of his frequent disruptions in class he'd been to see me more than once. After sitting down, opening my laptop, and pounding away on the keys as I did the observation, the boy kept glancing at me. He obviously was being very careful to have his glances be at times the teacher was writing on the white board so that he wouldn't garner her negative reaction for not paying attention. After five or six minutes of this he just couldn't help himself; he had to speak to me.

"Are you here for me? I didn't do anything."

I waited a second and then whispered, "No, I am here to observe Mrs. Smith."

"So, I am not in trouble?"

"No, should you be?"

"No; so you are Mrs. Smith's boss, and you're just watching her?"

This conversation was done in complete secrecy. He was very adept at noticing when Mrs. Smith's back was turned so he could sneak it in without being noticed. I reiterated that I was observing her doing her job and was not there to watch him and asked him to stop talking and pay attention to the lesson.

He did so for a few minutes but I could see the wheels turning and he kept glaring back at me. A bit later, when he saw Mrs. Smith actively helping another student, he turned to me, glared almost angrily and literally pointed a finger at me and said, "Mr. Atwood, you need to understand that Mrs. Smith does a great job teaching every single day and cares about us. I know because I am here every day."

Mrs. Smith was understandably surprised to hear later that such a troublesome student had defended her.

The Screwdriver

Students were allowed water bottles with healthy drinks during the academic day at one high school where I worked. These included water, Gatorade, juices, etc., but not Coke, Pepsi, or other unhealthy soft drinks. I got a tip from a student that a certain group of students were mixing vodka with their orange juice.

Along with the school resource officer (SRO) I brought several students in that were carrying orange juice in water bottles. If they were 18, we could search the bottles without having the parent present. If they were under 18 we had to call a parent in before going further, if a criminal charge could be the outcome. A half a dozen or so were caught and appropriately dealt with. If any were also student athletes, they lost the privilege of being on a school team.

Of course, once some students are caught doing something like this the word spread likes wildfire. The good news is that students stop doing it for fear of being caught. In the course of dealing with the ones we did catch, a common name kept coming up. The student they mentioned was supposedly the biggest offender – the distributor of the vodka. We didn't see him carrying any water bottles with juice that day. However, I kept an eye on him and the next day he was, in fact, carrying a juice-filled bottle. As an 18 year old, a legal adult, his parents did not have to be present. He was brought into my office and he submitted voluntarily to a search.

The bottle did not smell of alcohol. But as the supposed ringleader of the vodka distribution, he was given a Breathalyzer. He blew a .000 so no alcohol was present. He was quite comfortable and smug through the entire process, knowing he was in the clear. My gut feeling was he had gotten wind of this and opted to play it safe versus carrying and drinking in school. He was thanked for his cooperation and sent on his way.

Within an hour his father landed in my office. The dad was very unreasonable and swearing up a storm. How dare we single out his son and make such a wild and crazy accusation? His son didn't drink alcohol. Without using any names of course, when I was able to get a word in edgewise, I explained how it had all played out. How it had come to us and that we had to follow up with those suspected and accused. We couldn't just turn a blind eye to the accusations.

I told him how his son's name kept coming up among those who were drinking and had said he was the provider of the vodka. The dad angrily wanted me to tell him those students' names, which of course I refused to do. That I wouldn't divulge the names made him even angrier. I was making it up because I had a vendetta against his son and was singling him out and trying to slander his name.

This was certainly not the first time I had dealt with his son. The boy had been in the fray with many disciplinary issues, and the parent's response was always the same –zero accountability. The more I explained protocol and procedure based on why we had reasonable suspicion, the angrier he became. Eventually, I asked the dad to leave, telling him his son was not being charged with possession or distribution.

His response, as he left swearing on the way out, was that he was going to get a lawyer and sue us for unreasonable search and seizure. I always followed the rules to the letter and knew he didn't have a leg to stand on, since his son volunteered the search of the water bottle. I never heard another word about it, which was often the case. If I had a ten-dollar bill for every parent who said they were going to sue me, I'd have collected a great many ten dollar bills during my career.

A while later some pretty reliable students told me that the son said his dad wouldn't give him anymore vodka because he had been caught distributing, so he could no longer provide. If that was true then not only was the son guilty, but the dad had been providing alcohol to minors.

The Escaping Breast

In my office there were three chairs. One was an old, broken-down cloth chair. It just enveloped you when you sat in it. I hesitated to get rid of it because, unlike the other two hard plastic and metal chairs, it was very comfortable. The athletic director was sitting in this comfy chair when a student came into my office with a complaint.

This 17-year-old girl felt the athletic director had handled a discipline issue poorly. She'd asked to talk to me about the incident between herself and another girl with the athletic director present.

Now Mr. H never got rattled, and he also took great pride in his reputation as a prankster. No one could embarrass him, but he took great delight in rattling his colleagues.

As the student was telling the story of the incident she became more and more animated and agitated. At one point, she swung her arm with a gesture and the pencil she was holding flew out of her hand and landed at the feet of the athletic director.

In a split second she reached down to pick it up just as Mr. H leaned forward in the chair to get it. Unfortunately, when the young woman leaned down to grab the pencil, one of her breasts escaped the confines of her shirt, a mere foot or so from Mr. H's face. She swooped up the pencil, stood back up, continuing to tell me her side of the story.

Mr. H embodied the proverbial deer-in-the-headlights with no idea what to say or do. The girl went on, oblivious to the fact her breast had been inches from his face.

In about five or six seconds, which seemed like an eternity, she realized what had happened, and without missing a beat, tucked it back inside her shirt, continuing her story, seemingly unshaken by the escape.

When she finished, I thanked her for her input, and told her I would discuss it with Mr. H, asking him if he had anything to say before I sent her back to her study hall. For the first time since I'd known him, he was absolutely speechless.

The Rats Leaving the Ship

At the high school level, unfortunately, drug use is a problem. My high school's discipline policy had users, once caught, suspended and dealers suspended pending a board hearing on possible expulsion as well as law enforcement involvement.

We'd been investigating a boy, a senior who allegedly had been dealing prescription pills like oxycontin for quite some time. As a senior he was of age. We got a tip that he would hide pills in highlighters and give his customers the highlighter. He had gotten so brazen that he allegedly would do it in front of staff in classes, at lunch, etc., under the guise of giving a friend a highlighter.

We got this information from another student. The suspect, at the time was at the vocational center in a neighboring town ten minutes away across the river. I made a plan with the local police to meet the vocational bus as it pulled up to the high school. The schedule was such that all vocational students were due back shortly. We allowed all the students off the bus except for our suspect. We took him to my office to be questioned and possibly searched. It played out just as I had expected. The student was caught red handed with drugs in a few highlighters.

The bus driver asked me to climb into the bus and walk up the aisle looking at the floor in front of each seat. In doing so I saw a wide assortment of cigarettes, pipes, marijuana baggies, a couple of knives, etc., probably some twenty or so items all together. Obviously students panicked when they saw me and a police officer waiting for the bus and ditched all they were carrying.

However, the student we questioned and searched hadn't dumped his half a dozen highlighters with drugs in them. Apparently he figured we'd be clueless about the highlighters and he didn't want to lose out on all that inventory or risk us discovering them on the bus with their hidden contents.

Teenage Sexual Pranks

Teenagers can sexualize almost anything; sex seems to be on their minds constantly. Yet they often don't have the knowledge base that they think they have about that topic.

I had to address one fellow at my high school for what he deemed "an honest mistake." His girlfriend was five foot five inches tall, an attractive young lady with long straight brunette hair and a slender figure. Ms. A, a young teacher, matched the same description. So when the student walking down the hall saw a figure he determined was his girlfriend, he came up behind her and swatted her on the bottom.

Ms. A wheeled around with a look of shock on her face. She told me later that she is positive that look was likely topped by the shock on the boy's face when he saw whose bottom he'd smacked.

Another boy was sent to my office just prior to the Christmas break for wearing an inappropriate belt buckle. The thing had mistletoe on it. When I tried to explain how offensive this was he escalated until it got to the point that I told him he would be suspended and sent home if he continued to refuse to take the belt buckle off.

This didn't faze him in the least. When I told him I'd be calling his mother and wouldn't that be embarrassing for him, he said, "Go ahead and call her." She was the one who'd given it to him.

Sure enough his mother defended him to the hilt; she thought it was funny and cute. In fact, her response was verbally obscene, attacking me personally. The boy was suspended anyway.

Another 18-year-old reported being sexually

harassed by a 17- year- old girl. When I asked him to be more specific he told me that since he had turned 18 the girl had been pressuring him to go out and rent porn videos for her to watch. Being underage she couldn't do it herself.

Still another boy had been taking cell phone photos up girls' short skirts and trying to sell them.

Then there was the group of seniors who had a "freshman list", young girls they deemed attractive. The challenge was to see who within the group could bed down with the most girls on the list.

Mr. P, a teacher in his late 20's, 6'2" tall, dark hair, single, and attractive was a problem at the high school because so many junior and senior girls swooned over him. It was obvious to him that some of his students were attracted to him, but he handled it very professionally until one fateful day.

He came to my office white as a ghost, obviously shaken, and nervous; something had really rocked him. He asked if he could see me privately. When we spoke he told me about a senior girl who had been flirting and he just didn't know what to do. The student, who always sat in the front row of his class had shown up this day with no underwear on. Whenever he looked out at the class she opened her legs.

"I'm afraid to address it because if I do she's going to know I looked, and so will her parents if I involve them." Here's how I fixed it. Mr. P was one of two people in his department. It was he and a 62-year-old woman teacher. She had 18 students and he had 22 for that class. I "randomly" needed to even out the class sizes to "help students" get more academic attention by distributing student loads evenly among the two teachers.

This was what I told her parents when they questioned their daughter being moved. It was the same class with the same curriculum. I told Mr. P if that didn't cure it and things got worse, we would have no choice but to involve the parents and address it head on. Thankfully, that never became necessary.

The Kindergarten "Accident"

Mrs. D called the office from her first grade classroom to say she was sending Michael to the office as he had wet his pants and was very upset. He wanted to see me she said, because he was too embarrassed to see the school nurse and wanted a man to help him.

He got to my office, crying with the intensity that makes young children have to suck in a breath as they are speaking because they are so distraught. It was standard practice at the elementary school to buy sweatpants, underwear, socks, mittens, winter hats and a variety of other things students needed, and store them in the closet in the nurses office for just such an emergency.

I took Michael into the bathroom and gave him clean things to replace his urine-drenched clothing. He said he could clean up and change without help, so I waited outside the door, asking him a couple of times if everything was ok. He said yes, and although I heard an occasional sob through the door, the intensity was diminishing rapidly. It had stopped by the time he came out.

I suggested he stay in my office for a few minutes to compose himself before going back to his classroom. He was glad to have that option and sat in a chair while I went back to work. When it was clear that he'd calmed down, I asked him a question.

"Michael, you have been in Mrs. D's class since September and this is December. You also were here all last year in kindergarten and didn't have an accident.

Mrs. D has a bathroom right in her classroom. Why do you think you had an accident?"

With a completely straight face and as serious as a heart attack, Michael responded. "Mr. Atwood, I waited too long to go, then someone was ahead of me, and then here's the worst part, when I got in the bathroom, my winkie was in a knot and by the time I got it straightened out, it was too late."

When I later told Mrs. D Michael's explanation, she laughed, saying "I guess he's going to make somebody happy some day."

Good Morning Meeting

In many kindergarten classroom things get crank-ing with a morning meeting. The meeting outlines the day and helps them stay organized. As any kindergarten teacher can tell you, without solid, concrete structure things can digress into something like herding cats when it comes to five year olds.

The morning meeting also teaches students to be kind and to treat each other with dignity and respect, getting to know and be comfortable speaking in front of their classmates. Socialization is just as critical to teach at this level as the academics, particularly when far too many youngsters come to school without these basic social skills.

Ms. F invited me to join her kindergarteners at their morning meeting early in my first year as principal in their school. Everyone sat in a circle on the rug, each, in turn, shaking their neighbor's hand and saying "good morning, Sarah, how are you today" etc. and going around the circle. I was sitting in the circle as well. Mary turned to me and looked into my eyes with a completely innocent and nervous look. She offered her tiny hand to me and then said shyly, " Good Morning Mr. ASSWOOD, how are you today?"

Not one of the five year olds picked up on it, but Ms. F certainly did: her smirk as she bit her bottom lip was a dead give away.

When the circle was complete, and Ms. F started to give instructions for the next activity, little Mary said to me with the sincerity and caring of a professional counselor, "It's ok, Mr. Atwood, everybody gets nervous the first time they do morning greeting."

Later that day when I walked in to get my lunch out of the teacher's room refrigerator, Ms. F saw me come in and immediately burst into laughter. I just smiled, grabbed my lunch, and retreated.

The Wanderer

Five-year-olds, by themselves, unsupervised in a hallway immediately got my radar up, so I was surprised to see a kindergartener out wandering the halls. He was a transfer student who had come in well into the school year. But his teacher was sharp as a tack and had eagle eyes in the back of her head, so I was doubly surprised he'd gotten out.

When I got close enough he spoke to me first. It was obvious he had been in this situation before, but didn't know who I was. He spoke right up:

"What is your name and where are you supposed to be right now?"

Snack Time

Students had a choice to bring a snack from home or get a free, healthy snack from the school. After all, it was the parent's right to give their child whatever snack they wanted. So I was surprised when a concerned kindergarten teacher sent a child's snack bag to my office, saying "Please take a look at it and let me know if you disagree."

Expecting to see a caffeine and sugar filled soft drink or red bull and a candy bar, or some other thing where I would have to again have a conversation with this kindergarten teacher about judging a parent's choice, I opened the bag and pulled out a small plastic-wrapped package.

It was a condom.

I promptly called the teacher's classroom and told her she made the right call. I then asked her to be sure the child got one of the school snacks. I assumed the story would end there.

It did not even cross my mind that "little Johnny" would go home and tell his mother that the teacher would not let him have his snack from home, that the teacher took it away and made him have a school healthy snack instead.

The mom landed in my office before school started the next morning. To say she was angry would be a huge understatement. I'll just leave it at that and not go into the colorful language or the furious "how dare you take my child's snack away?" I was able to convince her to calm down enough to get her into my office to "discuss the decision." All I had to do was give her what had been taken.

I will always remember the look on her face. She immediately blamed her husband who had packed the snack. She grabbed the condom and left. There was no apology for the obscenities. Unfortunately, there rarely is.

The Star Wars Light Saber

One day Ms. M, a first grade teacher, called me while I was meeting with the town manager. She was sending a boy to me because he took out the Star Wars light saber that he had brought from home. I immediately had my feathers ruffled and barked back at her, "You know the rule, take the light saber away, give it back to him at the end of the day with a warning that we'll call his parents if it happens again. I don't need to be involved with this."

Ms. M defied me. "No, he's definitely headed your way right now. You need to handle this one." She then hung up; I was not pleased to say the least.

The town manager and I were not far from finishing all we needed to discuss. I explained to him what had just happened, he chuckled a little, and we tackled the two remaining big ticket items we needed to discuss.

By the time he left, Jimmy was in the outer office waiting to see me. I brought him in, and started explaining the rules about distracting behavior, then asked him to take it out of his back pack and give it to me. He took the Star Wars light saber out, hit a button and it lit up. It also had a very distinctive humming sound from the batteries and a certain slight curvature.

He swung it around making appropriate light saber sound effects and said "isn't it cool Mr. Atwood?"

"Where did you get it, Jimmy?" I asked.

"Out of my mother's night stand."

By now it is likely each of you as readers have gleaned a clear picture of what this light saber really was. I took it from him and told him I would be calling his mom instead of giving it back at the end of the day.

He balked at that, but I explained this was more of a distraction, so I would be calling his mother. After he left my office, I imagined telling this mother that her son had brought her vibrator to school.

How the hell do you start that conversation? Finally, I called the mother, but thankfully her answering machine picked up. I left her a message that told her that her son had brought something from home, took it out in class, and it became a huge distraction. I asked that she please come by before 5 p.m. and pick it up.

As luck would have it, I had an IEP (Individual Education Plan) meeting after school for a special education student. I put the vibrator in a bag and without telling the secretary what it was, I left it with her in case "Ms Jones" came by to retrieve it while I was at the meeting.

When I got back the secretary asked me what was in the bag. Apparently the mom came in, literally grabbed the bag and left without a word. Probably her son had told her what he'd taken.

I never again heard from the mother. Additionally, from then on, at school functions such as the Holiday music concert, and other like functions, she avoided me whenever she saw me.

Beaten Up By a Five Year Old

Anyone who has worked with very young children can tell you that five-year-olds sometimes crave closeness to their teachers. This can lead to unsolicited hugs, sneezing into the face of people, and other things that, as they get a little older, they will come to realize isn't acceptable social behavior.

I liked to greet students at the door as they came in from the morning recess, speaking to them by name or making a personal comment like "How was the Little League game last night?"

The kindergartners might run up and hug me. One morning I stood talking with a teacher, greeting only students who spoke to me as I continued this conversation. I didn't notice a little girl who always gave me a hug, running full speed toward me, and head butted me in, let's just say, a sensitive area below the waist.

I was looking directly into the face of the teacher when this happened, and as she later told me, the half smile on my face immediately went to a horrified grimace, and I literally was dropped to my knees. I gave the child a brief hug, and she gleefully scampered off toward her classroom. I was having a hard time catching my breath; that particular pain is not something men can adequately describe to their female colleagues.

In about 15 seconds or so when I could muster it, I looked up at the teacher who had one hand over her mouth trying desperately to fight back laughter. She said through her hand, "We'll finish this later," as she walked away. I struggled to my feet and very gingerly got to my office.

I was apparently walking funny as the school secretary said, "Mr. Atwood, did you hurt your back?"

I was only able to mumble a muffled, "No." I shut my office door, sat in my chair and did absolutely nothing for the next 20 minutes or so. I recovered, although at one point, I quite literally thought I was going to throw up. Yes, yes indeed, I was beaten up by a five year old.

The Curse

We had a rule at my high school that the girls' dresses had to reach their fingertips. One mother became angry when her daughter was told her dress was too short, and that she would have a consequence if it was worn again.

The mother came to my office after school that day and was angry. Though I explained the reason for the rule, she did not agree, saying it was not her daughter's fault that she has "unusually short arms"; the dress could not possibly extend to her fingertips.

Surely, I said, her daughter must have pants or longer dresses or shorts that met the requirement.

"It doesn't matter if she does or doesn't. She will wear that dress and if she gets a consequence I will put a curse on you."

You can't talk rationally with irrational people.

The Hallway Pass

Teacher's all have their own style. Each had their own way of handling classroom management, and how they followed rules. Some were very black and white, while others saw gray and reasons for some latitude based on mitigating factors. For example, it's hard to be worried about doing your math homework when you are hiding in a bedroom closet trying to avoid a beating from your mom's latest drunken boyfriend.

Mrs. B was an "old school" teacher who went by the book each and every time. It was her way or the highway. She was a retired teacher whom we called on often to substitute teach for us. Students came to realize her hard–core stance pretty early on.

A new English teacher had been hired right out of college, 23 or so, enthusiastic and energetic. One morning early in the school year Mrs. B encountered this new teacher in the hall. She stopped and asked where his hallway pass was.

"Oh, " he said, "I'm a teacher here." She was having none of that. The more he insisted the angrier she got, telling him there would be consequences, not only for being in the hall without a pass, but also for lying.

Gross Events and Irrational Notes

There's a reason for the rule "no running in the hallways". A colleague was responding at a run to a volatile situation in a classroom. Unfortunately, a custodian had just been told that someone had vomited in that hallway and was on his way. Turning the last corner my colleague slipped in the vomit like he was on ice and landed flat on his back dead center in the mess. Just the sight of him with chunks hanging off was gross enough, not to even mention the smell. Once he got to the room the problem in the classroom took a back seat when they saw and smelled him.

At the end of a school year, students completely empty their assigned lockers. After they were gone for the summer custodial staff checks each locker to be sure it was empty and do necessary cleaning. One custodian, who was pretty tough and could handle about anything, became sick to her stomach when she opened one locker to find a partially decomposed rat in the locker.

Another custodian found a half empty can of sardines upside down in the locker.

Some students left nothing in lockers and used them very little, if at all. My suspicion was lockers like this had been abandoned much earlier in the year. A half eaten peanut butter and jelly sandwich turned up in one, with very colorful mold on it from green to black and in between.

A statistic from the State Principal Association showed that if a student misses 18 days of school for any reason it generally equates to a year's worth of academic growth being lost. That's pretty powerful stuff, but unfortunately it didn't cut much ice with some parents.

Here are a few notes, excuses for absence:

"Johnny was not in school yesterday because he had to go fishing with his dad."

"Jimmy was not in school yesterday because he had to go get his car out of the shop."

" Sarah was not in school this morning because she babysat our friend's kids."

" Sally walked out of detention yesterday and left early because she had a hair appointment."

" Suzy was not in school yesterday because we went shopping in Portland."

"Amy was home in pain yesterday because some dumb ass slammed her bad ankle in the door on Wednesday during the fire drill."

"Tom was at home yesterday because he needed a day to think."

" Jennifer was out of school last week because she had to babysit her brothers and sisters while we went on vacation to Florida."

"Mary was out of school yesterday because we went shopping for her prom dress."

" Peter was out yesterday because his car was dirty and needed to be washed."

" Andy will be out tomorrow for a haircut."

" Abby's sister is home for a visit and we are going to a movie two hours away so Abby needs to be dismissed early from school today."

" Jack won't be in school tomorrow because we just found out that his sister is pregnant."

These certainly speak to the priority some people assigned to school time.

The Ed Tech Sick Days

Both classroom teachers and ed techs, by contract, have a certain number of sick days each year which can accumulate year to year. It's a great benefit, particularly for anyone who has a devastating injury or disease. Unfortunately, some people abuse that benefit and use them as personal days, not sick days. Some were caught out and about doing things they wouldn't be doing if they were actually sick.

One ed tech not only called out sick, but she also wrote a sick note for her high school age daughter and a few of her daughter's friends. She took these teen-agers out of school and on a shopping trip to the Maine Mall in Portland without the knowledge of their parents and was caught doing so.

What if a parent had come to school to get their child? What if they'd been in an accident?

Another ed tech took sick time on multiple occasions *and* wrote a sick note for his children so the entire family could compete in horseback riding competitions. He was caught at this as his children were telling their friends why they really would be out of school, and word got back to administration.

This type of behavior also did not give educators a good reputation in the community when taxpayers saw these people out and about in the community when they were supposedly sick.

Another bad public relations move was when sick days were taken during professional development days. School was not in session, but professional development days are just that, and staff is required to attend.

No wonder some community members and parents saw "professional development" as code for goof off days. Luckily, this type of abuse is the exception; most educators are very professional.

The Hot Fudge Sundae

At the two elementary schools where I was the principal we participated in an event called the "Darlings Ice Cream Truck". Darlings is a local car dealership; they send an ice cream truck to schools and sometimes other events once a year to give away free ice cream to support some activity or fund raiser the school was doing.

This is a great public relations event for the car dealership and certainly gets their name out there in a positive way. The ice cream was indeed free to the students, but there was also a donation box. Every penny taken in was given back to the school. With 350 students, hundreds of parents and relatives dropped by to pick up or drop off students and were solicited to participate and get a free ice cream.

There were a variety of flavors as well as a frozen yogurt. I used the ice cream truck as a tool in the teacher's tool bag to help with behavior. If a student had been suspended or had a bad track record they were ineligible to get their free ice cream when the truck came around.

Each grade in turn would go down to the truck to get an ice cream and then back to their classroom late in the afternoon. The school was on a busy street, so we put the Free Ice Cream sign out by the road in order to get the attention of passing motorists.

The Darlings people also had three ice cream suits – an ice cream sandwich, a regular ice cream, and a hot fudge sundae with the hat being the cherry on top. Staff and volunteer parents wore them to attract attention from the passing public. I wore the hot fudge sundae suit.

The truck would be at the school for about two hours or so in the afternoon and coincided with dismissal so as to get optimal parental involvement. It was a fun event and netted funds for the school that I used to support other positive events for students. One was a Christmas time trip to the local theatre to watch an animated Disney movie, again with students eligible to go based on behavior.

The theatre gave me a price of $4 a head that included popcorn and a drink. We'd leave at 8:15 or so for the theater and be back before lunch. With nearly 8 in 10 students coming from homes where income levels made them eligible for free/reduced lunch, it was likely the only time in the entire year these kids would get a chance to see a movie in a theatre.

So I wore the hot fudge sundae suit. Students (staff and parents too) got a charge out of seeing the principal dressed up in a funny looking suit.

One parent, Mrs. T, was a strong member of the parent/teacher group; she volunteered to work on many events at the school and substituted occasionally as well. Additionally, she would help out in the office and stayed in tune with her child's educational progress. Whenever I needed help with an event she never said no.

The first year I ran the Darling's Ice Cream truck event Mrs. T volunteered to dress up in one of the suits. She went out by the road, making a spectacle of herself and encouraging other parents to get a free ice cream and make a small donation. Bear in mind that this was my first year at the school, and even though I knew her, I didn't know her all that well yet.

We stood together next to the truck, having a good time as students were making comments about our outfits. A second grade girl came up to me and giggling, said, "Mr. Atwood, I like your hot fudge sundae suit."

"I'm glad you like it," I said, "I hope you enjoy your ice cream. You deserve it as you have had a great year so far."

She replied, "I'd really like to have your cherry," and scampered off to get back in line.

I glanced over at Mrs. T in her ice cream sandwich suit. She grinned and whispered to me, "When was the last time you heard someone say that to you? I bet around the time you were sixteen."

What was I supposed to say to that? I just smiled and pressed on with the business at hand.

Embarrassing The Boss

The health teacher and the physical education teacher were both involved in an incident where a student badly disrespected and swore at them. I'd handled the situation per our disciplinary code, then went to see the two teachers and explain the outcome. These two women had dealt with the student's mother before, a person who was both volatile and confrontational, and both were apprehensive because no matter what "little Johnny" did, the mother never accepted what happened. She always blamed the staff involved; her little Johnny was never responsible.

I went to see these two teachers to tell them that I'd taken care of it; they wouldn't have to deal with this irrational mother. Coming into the P.E. office I shut the door behind me, not realizing it was in the locked position. I told them what action I'd taken, and what the consequences were, as well as when they could expect to see little Johnny back.

There was probably a 15-minute discussion about the incident and how his attitude and disrespect had been seen by other staff as well. Then I headed for the door. But the door wouldn't open. I fiddled with the button, but no luck. By now those two were making remarks about my incompetence with a simple door lock. After a couple of laughs I encouraged them to come open it. They tried, but just like myself they could not get the door open. We were locked together in this room.

After 10 minutes or so of futile struggling with the door I called the office. But as soon as I started talking with the secretary my fellow captives began in the most seductive tones:

"Oooh, Ahhhh"

"Yes, oh yes"

"That's it"

"Oh that feels so good"

"Oh Terry don't stop."

So that's what they were up to! They got so loud I had to practically shout for the secretary to hear me. She certainly could hear them!

Meanwhile, she didn't understand why I couldn't unlock the door. Finally, I just said, "Send Jim down here!" and hung up. I gave my teacher "friends" an earful once off the phone, but they were laughing so hard the tears were streaming down.

It only took the custodian a couple of minutes to figure out the lock was broken, and that he had to go retrieve some tools. I had to endure a few more minutes of this abuse while he was gone, and the more frustrated I got, the more they kept it up.

Of course Jim heard them when he returned, so he knocked! And of course I promptly responded. In three or four minutes he had the door open and I was finally out of this torture.

Thankfully the secretary knew full well the prankster capacity of these two teachers, and Jim and I had a great relationship as well. However, he later told me he wasn't sure if he should knock or not and asked me what was going on.

Don't hit the "Send" Button

I learned fairly early on that before sending out any email correspondence that you have to read your emails for errors. One of the tricks that I use before sending out correspondence is to read my email backwards. That forces you to read each word versus groups of words; missing even one single letter can have poor results.

Young Ms. S sent me the following:

"Good morning, I wanted to let you know that I have my email account now and would like to be added to the email list serve to receive the daily announcements. I would like to stop in your office after school today to discuss a few things if possible. Yesterday went very well, I have a wonderful group of kids! Thank you, Mary Smith. "

I wrote back:

"I have two meetings after school today already. One is at 2:15 with the custodians and the other at 3 pm at the Superintendent's office for the Elementary Level Proficiency Based Education team meeting. I'll ensure you get added to the school email lust serve. Tomorrow after school is a better time to meet if that works for you. Terry"

I did not, because of the hair-on-fire day that was way too typical, read the email backwards. If I had done so I am sure I would have caught the word 'lust' versus the word 'list'. Depending on spell check to save you won't help with a correctly spelled word.

Thankfully, Ms. S had a sense of humor and rather than share my mistake with others who would have taken great delight in roasting me for it, she chose to discreetly point it out, which I appreciated.

Read it backwards, no exceptions!

Out of the Mouths of Babes

A third grader writing during a unit on Canadian History:

"These Inuit Indians made money during the gold rush. They did very well while panning for gold. These prostitutes had a great thing going."

Did he mean *prospectors*?

"Prostitutes came and went and followed the gold rush wherever it took them. They were good at it and many of them made lots of money."

Another third grader said to her teacher:

"I can't use the living room space to spread out and work on my science project."

"Why?" asked the teacher.

"Because, behind the couch is where my mom and dad have the grow lamps that are on all the time for their special plants, and we get yelled at if we go near them so I couldn't move the couch back to make room."

From a first grader:

"My mom has a new boyfriend. I really like him and he's not one of my uncles this time."

And a second grader when the teacher was going over something that dealt with different socioeconomic classes wrote: "What is it like to be porn?"

When I was principal of an elementary school I worked out a deal with a local theater to take the entire K-6 school to the movies to see a holiday movie. The teachers and ed techs went as well to supervise their classes. As long as we as a staff did all the prep and clean up afterward, the theater gave me a great rate of $4 a head, which included popcorn and a (non-soda) drink.

The kids loved it, and they knew they were only

eligible to go if they had had a good first half year behaviorally. In this school 80% of the students were eligible for free/reduced lunch; this might be their only chance to go to a movie theatre. We left after breakfast and were back to the school by lunch, so it was very manageable with eight buses, and typically went very well.

Upon return, several teachers had students write a thank you note to me. They came into my in box in the office, and of course, I read each one.

From a sixth grader:

"Thanks Mr. Atwood for taking us to the movies. I really liked the popcorn and the vodka."

Not every student wrote a thank you note. Some just wrote what was on their minds.

From a first grader, clearly having trouble with his Bs and Ds:

"When you ride a dick, you should always wear a helmet. "When his teacher came up to me after school as I was reading the notes, she had such a grin on her face I knew something was up.

I was visiting a second grade classroom during snack time when one very social little girl came up to me.

"Do you like goldfish Mr. Atwood?"

"Yes, but I'm not hungry right now, thanks anyway."

"I wasn't asking to share with you because it's a school rule not to share food from home at snack time because of germs and allergies people might have. You made the rule Mr. Atwood and you don't know about it?"

Yes, this kid called me out on one of my rules!

A kindergartner, said, "Mr. Atwood, you are looking good today." His drawn out inflection on "good" showed he was well-versed in the art of buttering up.

Like many communities in Maine, the town where I was the principal at an elementary school had a problem with ticks. Students were told to tell an adult if they had a tick on them and the school nurse, if available, would remove it and notify parents.

Since school nurses are often shared between district buildings, our nurse was often not in. When little Ellie came to the office and said she had a tick, I asked her if it was in a private area.

"Oh no, it's not on me; my doll has a tick."

A third grader wrote about her summer vacation, a trip to Virginia. Except she'd written "Vagina" for "Virginia".

Another student wrote "penis" when he meant "pen". Most elementary teachers can share similar stories.

Occasionally I had to fill in on recess duty. This school had two playgrounds – one for K-2 and another for grades 3-6. One day when the younger children had been sent to the older kids' playground, I was supervising first grade recess. One little boy ran over to report some words had been scratched into the swing set. He came with me in lock step to point it out.

"See Mr. Atwood, the older kids don't know how to spell can't." Needs no further explanation.

As part of our teacher evaluation we survey students. There was a district-wide survey for grades K-2 and another for 3-6. The K-2 survey used a smiley face for agreement or an upside down smiley face for disagreement. Here are a few of the statements from the K-2 survey form.

My teacher gives me help when I need it.
My teacher shows me how to do new things.
I know what I am supposed to do in class.
I am able to do the work in class.
I feel safe in my classroom.

One first grader wrote in the comment section: "Mrs. Smith can not do a hand stand."

I'm not sure the viewpoints of five to seven year olds were always rational. For example, if Tommy had to be reprimanded the morning of the survey he might slam the teacher on the survey. Certainly it was not on his mind what this teacher had helped him to accomplish all year long.

Here are a couple of examples of first grade writing (spelling and grammar errors corrected):

"I feel that a pig is a horrible pet. First they are crazy. Second, they might poop. One last reason is that they smell. I hope you agree that a pig is a bad pet."

And:

"Dear Mr. Atwood, do you chop wood? Did you know that your name ends with wood? Therefore, it would be appropriate if you chopped wood. Just so you know, me and Brik are going to have a snowball fight at lunch recess today."

A first grader, sent on an errand to the gym teacher during a sixth grade P.E, class, asked loudly:

"Mrs. Smith sent me down here to ask if you have two balls."

A six-year-old boy was crying in his classroom, and obviously bothered by something. The teacher called me to say that the boy was on his way to see me. The boy had said his mother was very sick and he was afraid she was dying.

In the privacy of my office the boy said, "I think my mom is dying." and burst into uncontrollable tears. I asked him why he thought that.

"Well, when I go to bed every other night or so something happens. Sometimes it takes me a while to fall asleep. After I have been in bed for maybe an hour it happens, I hear her, I hear my mom, she's screaming and screaming. Sometimes she yells words too, like Oh God, Oh God!!"

By this time I had a clear picture of what was really going on.

"Timmy, I don't think your mom is dying." He immediately seemed to be calming down and tears dwindled.

"What should I do?"

I told him to talk to his mom that night and tell her exactly what he had told me about why he thought she might be dying.

"She likely will tell you that she's fine and can explain."

I am positive the boy did as I suggested because whenever the mom was in the school after that she avoided me like the plague.

Then there was the following conversation overheard in a fourth grade classroom:

"I am really worried about my daddy. He didn't come home last night."

Said with the sincerity of a pastor the other child replied, "Oh, you don't need to worry about him, he's fine. He was over to my house all night visiting my mom."

Stupid Parent Tricks

Most parents had a good working relationship with the school, finding what was best for their child's success and supported school decisions. However the percentage of parents that fought us every step of the way was growing at a scary rate by the time I retired.

You can't talk rationally with irrational people. No matter what hard evidence you provide them with you won't please them or have them see the point you are making. Once I came to this realization I just stopped wasting valuable time and energy on people I knew I was never going to win over.

I would matter-of-factly explain the circumstances, and the consequences of whatever happened involving their child and then stuck to my decision. After some time, people realized they might as well not bother to argue with me or try to get me to change my decision. If facts were clear I just made a decision and moved forward.

This is what it's like talking to irrational people: *If you are going down a river at 2 miles per hour and your canoe loses a wheel, how much pancake mix would you need to re-shingle your roof?* Yah, it's like that.

The rule was clear; parents could not drop off their child earlier than 7:40 am. The rationale was pretty basic and certainly clear. The outside morning recess duty teachers didn't start until 7:40 am. For the child's own safety, early drop off meant no supervision on the playground.

No one would want a child to fall off a slide or monkey bars and get hurt with no adult out there. Nor would anyone want an unsupervised child to be abducted. More than once in my career I had legally noncustodial parents threaten to abduct their child, not to mention even more sinister abduction possibilities.

Many times I had to remind parents of the rule, and even had a local sheriff speak to the ones who just ignored it. They would drop their child in the parking lot, tell them to go to the playground, and then leave.

Even after explaining it was for the child's own safety I would battle with parents on this until I figured out they were irrational. I also always warned them that law enforcement involvement was the next step.

One mom was quick to call and try to argue with me after a sheriff had told her it could be considered child endangerment if she kept doing it. "I drop her off at 7 am because I have to go to work."

"Then hire childcare," I said, "As I have told you before, we are educators not babysitters, and we don't want to risk your child's safety with no supervision."

That was it, and I made clear there was no further discussion. I always passed on the whole scenario ahead of time to my boss, the superintendent. Invariably the indignant parent would end up at his office, screaming there as well. Of course, this same mother would be quick to get to a lawyer's office to try and sue the school if her child got hurt unsupervised.

Then there was the parent who was constantly complaining that her child was being bullied at school and that the school was at fault for allowing this to happen. In fact this fourth grade boy had never reported to anyone that he was being bullied. Furthermore, upon investigation, I discovered that he was the perpetrator of bullying activity.

Occasionally, a student whom he bullied would retaliate and fight back, rather than reporting it to us, but otherwise this boy was the perpetrator. On more than one occasion he was suspended for physical aggression, usually on younger children. The mother typically posted on social media, after not being able to get his consequences overturned, that I was a terrible principal who suspended her son for being a victim of bullying. The school had cameras in common areas, the playground, cafeteria, hallways, etc. Often I could witness what he had done.

On one occasion, I showed the mother a clip of her son coming in from lunch recess. He came up behind another student and body slammed the younger student into the lockers, causing physical harm to his victim. His story to his mother was *he* had been body slammed, and he got consequences not the student who attacked him.

Of course, the mom landed in my office unannounced, screaming at this injustice. I invited her in to watch what had happened on my laptop. I could connect to any chosen camera and review footage. I suspected, once she saw the video, that she would be embarrassed at her son's lie, and maybe even apologize for swearing at me, etc.

I should have known better given my experience with this woman in the past. She said, after seeing her son clearly attack and hurt another child, "Well, since you never address him being bullied, he feels he has to take matters into his own hands because you never do."

At this point, I asked her to leave, taking her suspended son with her, letting her know when he could return. I spoke in a calm voice, just matter of factly telling her my decision. I learned early on to stay calm and not get into a screaming match, as in some cases that was what the parent wanted; then they could attack *me* for being unprofessional. I briefed my boss as I suspected she would go to him as she had in the past.

However, when she landed at the superintendent's office she asked to meet with the school board. When the superintendent's secretary asked if she'd like an appointment to talk to him, the mom responded, "hell no, the superintendent always covers Atwood's ass anyway." You can't talk rationally with irrational people.

I suspended a high school student for three days after he'd threatened bodily harm to a teacher, and then followed her home and egged her house. Her perceived atrocity was that she "gave him a failing grade that quarter". Of course he earned the grade he received. It was always the case that students earned an A, but somehow a teacher gave them an F.

The suspension meant the boy was ineligible to play on the basketball team for a period of time. Of course, as an adult, bodily threatening is a criminal activity and he could have been prosecuted. A three-day suspension and not playing ball for a while doesn't compare in terms of severity. Of course his father didn't see it that way. He showed up at a board meeting protesting loudly, that "suspending his son was like giving a shoplifter a death sentence."

That father was much more concerned about his son missing a basketball game than he was about the boy's academic downward spiral. Like many other parents I encountered he could not even tell you who their child's teacher or teachers were. At one elementary school where I worked and children had one teacher, some parents didn't even know what grade their child was in when they called to complain about a teacher, much less who the teacher was who was "giving" their child an F.

Placement meetings to figure out which teacher a child got was a logistical jigsaw puzzle, putting all the considerations together, not to mention getting a half dozen subs in to cover classes while the meetings took place. It was tedious and time consuming. I drafted a letter that went out to all parents, saying that it was critical a parent submit, in writing, by a deadline date, a specific academically sound request for student placement the following year, in other words, why they thought a certain teacher was a good fit for their child. To be with a friend or a cousin was not a legitimate reason. The letter went out weeks before the deadline, and it was made clear the deadline date was firm, typically the last day before spring break. We generally started those placement meetings the week after spring break and it would take all day for an entire week to finalize all grade levels at the school, which involved many man hours. Parent requests were honored if at all possible.

However, occasionally, for reasons the staff knew, they couldn't always be honored. If Susie was constantly fighting with Johnny for example, it was better to have them in separate classrooms. Additionally, we sent home placement information on the last day of school, which was also step-up day, the day students visited, for a short period of time, with the following year's teacher.

Invariably, there would be a dozen or so parents who did not do a placement request by the deadline. Sometimes weeks or even a month later they demanded an input to placement. Knowing all the work that went into placements, the assistant superintendent was very good about supporting me when I didn't bow down to late submissions that would require a ton of work that had already been done.

Additionally, there were parents who, after learning who their child had been placed with, demanded after the last day of school a different placement, even though they had never submitted a request. Unfortunately, even though I stuck to the placements that had been made, these unpleasant confrontations happened annually. Some of the ludicrous parent demands amazed me.

Smoking on school grounds reaped an automatic suspension of five days on a first offense. If the student was a student athlete, they were dropped from the athletic team.

A boy who had been caught smoking a swisher sweet cigar was suspended and dropped from an athletic team. His parents were so out of bounds in my office that I had to ask them to leave. Their view was they were okay with it, so why shouldn't the school be? When it became obvious the consequence was going to stand, they tried to bargain: "why can't he just do a detention?"

A mother wanted it stated in her fifth grader's IEP that the child could drink caffeinated coffee in all classes as "it helped the child study."

High schoolers were give detention if they were late to school three times in a quarter. The rationale for the rule was to instill being on time as a good work ethic. We certainly didn't want a student losing a job for constantly being tardy. "What's the big deal?" said the parents of a chronically late student. No amount of explaining the reason mattered. You can't talk rationally with irrational people.

A boy was given detention time for calling another student a pussy. The parent came in angry, saying "How do you know he wasn't calling him a cat?"

Then there was the mother who showed up to do the detention for her daughter when it became obvious that it was going to happen or she'd get a worse consequence.

A girl was sending threatening messages of bodily harm to another student. First her mother denied it. When I showed her the evidence, she shot back with "It was a text message so she didn't actually say it to her, so it wasn't a threat."

At high school athletic contests, either a school administrator or the athletic director had to be in attendance to pay officials, and take care of any problems that came up such as trouble with a game clock or students or parents that got out of hand. As unfortunate as it is, I had to deal with several out of bounds parents.

A dad was screaming and cursing at the officials during a girls' basketball game, "Hey, open your eyes ref, you're missing one hell of a game you asshole!" Other parents were cheering him on and this only fueled him. When I went to speak to him, other parents who knew how I operated and who had been a party to encouraging him, kind of slithered away and backed off as they heard our interchange.

"Mr. Jones, you need to calm down and be a better example to the kids, including your daughter. Please stop yelling and cursing at the officials."

"Fuck you, I paid my goddamn money, you can't throw me out of here."

"That's where you are wrong. I absolutely can, and that police officer over by the door will be asked to remove you bodily if necessary. Please avoid that embarrassment to you and your daughter. I'm giving you one last chance to knock it off. Am I clear?"

He did not say a word but slightly nodded his head. It wasn't five minutes later he slammed the official again with obscenity-laced insults. I immediately went up and asked him to leave. By now his buddies had abandoned him and were distancing themselves from him. Again he told me that I needed to go do something to myself that is anatomically impossible. I alerted the police officer we had hired to cover the event, and when the guy gave the officer a hard time he went out in hand cuffs in front of the crowd. Furthermore, he was banned for the rest of the season from attending games, given a do not trespass order, and told by the police if he showed up anyway he would be arrested.

Of course, that news spread like wildfire in the community, so one positive effect was it greatly diminished problems with out of bounds parents at basketball games the rest of that season. When the dad called later and asked to speak to me, he apologized and wanted to be allowed back. I did not do that for the remaining regular season games, but he was allowed back when the team made the playoffs. The worst part of this episode was how embarrassed his daughter was. She came and apologized the day after the incident for her father's behavior, which obviously had nothing to do with her. She was a good student and a strong athlete. It certainly was a shame when the 17-year-old was more mature than her dad.

Unfortunately, there are a few parents out there who believe that a school principal works for them and therefore must comply with any demand they make. Ideally, it should be a supportive partnership, built on trust. Of course all school administrators should listen to parent input, but ultimately the building principal has to make decisions based on the best decision for typically hundreds of students, not one at the expense of the many.

A principal should always try to work with parents, but when you get an unreasonable screamer who refuses to consider a different viewpoint, or listen to the rationale for a rule, then it occasionally becomes necessary to just make a decision and move on. Where can one go to see any professional such as a dentist, auto mechanic, plumber, doctor, anywhere, and angrily demand attention that very moment?

One day as I was in the middle of a formal teacher observation (a requisite yearly, hour-long meeting a principal has with each teacher) the office secretary paged me. She said a certain parent, whom I had had a series of negative interactions with before, was on her way in to see me and would be there in 30 minutes. Furthermore she had demanded that I be in my office when she arrived, saying "He goddamn better well be there when I get there." The secretary said I wouldn't be available for about 45 minutes.

"No, you tell him to have his ass in that office when I get there!"

When I finished the observation I went back to the office to find the mother waiting for me, and she was not displaying any more of a rosy disposition.

She immediately started screaming, saying that she'd told the secretary to have me in the office when she arrived.

I coaxed her into my office where her display was a bit less public. However, I left my door open so the secretary could hear the conversation so as to validate what was said. Of course, this was something else I learned through experience, not graduate school.

The woman could not be reeled in. She continued her screaming rant, attacking me personally and not getting to whatever her issue was. "Listen you fucking jerk, I pay my taxes, you work for me. When I tell you to be here, you better fucking be here."

"Actually I don't work for you. I work for the superintendent of schools and no you didn't pay taxes, so before I ask you to leave I will ask you to calm down and tell me your problem so that I can try to address it."

"I did too pay my taxes, I file them every year."

I then explained that income taxes don't fund public schools, property taxes do. I knew this family lived in a rented mobile home in a trailer park. She didn't actually pay any property taxes. Furthermore, I told her to please call ahead from now on and make an appointment to see me. "If you are told I am not available please honor that and I assure you I will schedule to see you as soon as I can." To her credit, she let me say that without yelling and interrupting.

She calmed down enough to tell me her son was being bullied and why wasn't I doing anything about it? I told her that her son had never once reported being bullied. I couldn't magically know about it and now that I do, I would talk to her son, get the particulars and investigate it. Her response, shocking I know, was "You ain't gonna do shit about it."

She left cursing all the way out. I would like to say that this type of interaction was uncommon but that would not be the truth. In fact, by the time I retired it had increased dramatically.

Of course, there was a reason her son had not reported being bullied. He had instigated it. He ended up with a consequence, and I invited his mother in to see a recorded video of a hallway incident where her son started something. When he poked the bull he got the horns so to speak. The victim retaliated after clearly trying to get her son to stop. Of course, the mother did not take me up on that offer. She just painted a false story on social media.

What was it that parents were really teaching their children with their behavior? One mother tried to bring a lawsuit when her child was let go from the basketball team. The daughter had been caught in school with alcohol in her water bottle. The suit of course had no legs, as playing high school sports is a privilege and not a right. The mother actually said to me, "Yes, so it was alcohol in the water bottle but you didn't actually have anyone see her drink from it so therefore you didn't actually catch her drinking so she should still be allowed to play."

Another parent said to me that his child's grade should be altered because he should be allowed to do some independent study work and get the grade back up. When that was denied the dad said, "If my kid was a football player, you would let him I'm sure."

When a student's academic performance was poor, his mother demanded that another student, a girl, be forced to sit in the back of the room because she was too sexy, and therefore was distracting her son. It was not his fault at all.

A father complained that he was tired of my "hauling" his kid into the office. I explained that when he son was in a scrape I had to talk to him. His problem was I was humiliating his son "hauling" him down to the office. His son had been blowing off homeroom attendance, so I called his first period class and asked him to stop in to see me during transition time to his second period class. What a horrendous embarrassment I had caused his son, at least that was the dad's view.

A mother drove up in a brand new car, was talking on a cell phone on her way in, and when she got off the phone was angry because "I can't afford gym shorts for my kid; why is he being forced to have gym clothing?"

Or the high schooler's mother angry at her daughter's detention for being late to school three times in a quarter: she came in screaming that "you're a fucking liar, I dropped my kid off yesterday at 7:15 am so no way in hell was she late for school since she didn't have to be in school till 7:30." When I explained that the girl may have been dropped off at 7:15 but she didn't go to homeroom where attendance is taken until well after both the warning bell and the late bell had sounded. Then the story changed; it was such a stupid rule because her daughter was in fact here on school grounds.

A student was suspended pending an expulsion hearing for dealing drugs. The parent was firm in saying "my kid doesn't sell or do drugs." However, the student had left school grounds to walk to the neighboring middle school to sell to an eighth grader and was caught red-handed doing so. All the evidence presented was completely ignored, and we were painted on social media as evil because we were keeping their child from getting an education without any reason.

There was a parent who wrote a false sick note for their child, and then the student was seen swimming at a local pool. Rather than admit the fabrication the parent said it was doctor-directed therapy. Of course when asked, no doctor's note was ever produced.

I was interrupted in the middle of a meeting, right after school one day by a young man with some sort of emergency. Turns out his Boston Bruins jersey had been stolen, and he demanded I start investigating right now. I told him I'd look into it first thing in the morning.

Twenty minutes later his dad called demanding the secretary get me out of the meeting to talk to him. When she tried to take a message his language turned so foul she came and got me. If I didn't start investigating the stolen jersey right now, he'd said, I'd be paying for it out of my own pocket. When she repeated that I was unavailable until morning, he called her a "stupid c---"

I had suspended a boy for very violent behavior, hurting much younger students and threatening staff with bodily harm. An emergency IEP was called to discuss the matter; these are the adults who showed up at the meeting. Pay close attention because it is hard to follow:

The boy's biological dad and biological mom, the biological mom's first girlfriend partner and biological mom's second female partner all came in together. When introductions were made it was clear that biological mom's first partner was there because she had left biological mom for biological dad, and the two of them were an item. All five children and these four adults lived in the same single-wide mobile home.

I had a parent who was stealing their child's meds and selling them.

A student was sent to school with a Bud Light to have at snack time.

A student missed the bus. When I asked him to call his parent for a ride home, he said he couldn't because they were gone to Florida this week on vacation.

This boy was nine years old and his younger sibling was seven. They had been left to fend for themselves.

I had a student sent to school in the same clothes all week long with feces dried on to his clothes and no socks and no underwear.

Very young children using extremely vulgar language as well as sexualized talk.

One boy told me his father showed him how to slit the throat on animals in case he needed to know how to protect himself.

A parent said to me "Fuck you, you fucking asshole, you always are picking on my kid. His smoking is an addiction, and he should be allowed to smoke on school grounds because he's addicted. Besides, I'm fine with him smoking."

Another pair of parents were upset that the principal had confiscated their son's school-issued laptop when porn sites were discovered. They actually said, "Please let him bring it home; we promise we won't let him use it." This begged the question: who was going to those sites on the machine while it was at home?

I had a steady stream of high drama in the high school from jealousy fights to retaliation, sometimes years after the fact. Girls calling each other the "C" word in school laptop email conversations, spray-painting another student's car, a sucker punch that resulted in a broken jaw, and even two parents threatening each other, blaming the other one's child for the problem.

I had a parent call me wanting me to take action against another parent who had called her at home and made threatening comments. In all these incidents we followed through with consequences, and called the Department of Human Services when warranted as we are mandated reporters.

Hell hath no fury like a teenage girl who feels she has been scorned. Just prior to school one morning there was an out of the blue sucker punch, followed up by a knock down, drag out, hair pulling, kicking, punching scratching fight between two high school girls. After they were broken up and calmed down they were interviewed separately about the fight to determine the root cause, and what actions would be taken from there.

The girl who started it said simply, "She looked at my boyfriend!"

The other girl said "Well she did x, y, and z back when we were freshman."

Yes, that's right, harboring resentment for relatively minor things two years earlier. Now for the really sad part. Both parents saw the other child as totally at fault. Bear in mind that the sucker punch victim got the upper hand, and while staff were trying to break things up, the victim was actively trying to fight after the first one had stopped.

On one occasion I had a parent angry and screaming because the first grade teacher cut up their child's watermelon into smaller slices so that the child could handle the slices better. They felt the child should have been allowed the knife to cut it up himself. After all, he was six years old now. They wanted the teacher fired over it. You can't talk rationally with irrational people.

It was policy in the elementary school that a student could not take a bus home other than their own without written parent permission. Nor could they leave campus after school and walk if they were a bus student. Once the written notice was received we would call the parent and verify. The rationale is simple. We needed to be sure parents knew their child's whereabouts.

Secondly, some students tried to go to a friend's house and not tell their parent they were doing so. Third, as scary as it sounds, there are bad folks in the world, including people who would abuse or harm children if the opportunity arouse.

There were registered sex offenders in the town and a few convicted pedophiles. It was astounding how many parents got angry that we didn't allow young students to walk or ride a different bus based on the child's word. They wanted the child to go somewhere else – to a babysitter, to grandparents', or a friend's house – but didn't believe they had to put it in writing.

No amount of explanation for the rule did any good so once I figured out those parent types we just followed the policy and they always complained loudly about it, sometimes claiming "they didn't have time" to write a note, a three or four sentence note to ensure their child's safety. They were also offended when we called to verify a note. "My child wouldn't forge a note."

I had a parent threaten to sue me because I wouldn't personally reimburse them for a hat that was stolen from their son. Frankly, I'd like to have $10.00 for every time I heard a parent say that they were going to sue me. When I (obviously) didn't reimburse them, saying we would continue to investigate and try to find the hat and the thief, they left my office calling me a fucking asshole.

One time a mother called, demanding to see me over a teacher she wanted to have charged with child abuse. That, of course, got my attention. I invited her in to give me details of the abuse because of course I would take that accusation seriously and investigate. The mom came in and wanted immediately to know when I would involve the police. I asked her to confide in me the accusations so that I could determine if it was appropriate to involve the police at this point. What was the child abuse?

"Mrs. Smith gave my son homework over school vacation. Vacation is for families to enjoy time with their children, and it is child abuse and criminal to demand my son do any work at all over vacation." She was completely serious. I know this is shocking, but I didn't involve the police. Then of course her anger was with me. I learned later she had called the superintendent's office because "I was so unprofessional."

I readily admit a grin when she explained the abuse. You can't talk rationally with irrational people.

This next one is a quote from a note a parent sent to her son's teacher. "Johnny was absent on Friday May 4th due to a combination of personal family matters and his extreme depression stemming from a long week of bullying and harassment that the school did not address. AGAIN, I would like to attempt to set up a meeting with the school and the parents of the children who are daily abusing my son verbally. School punishments seem to accomplish nothing so perhaps parental involvement is necessary to discuss the serious implications of the effects of Johnny's harassment."

I had dealt with this mother many times before. Her son had never reported harassment because whenever he was involved it was clear he was the initial aggressor. She was a screamer and irrational, and the last thing I was going to do was be the mediator between her and other parents. I told her we would not be calling a parent meeting here at school, but she was welcome to get names from her son and contact parents herself outside of the school environment.

Sometimes, at least fairly early in my administrator tenure, I was surprised at how people felt their child should not receive a consequence at all or just a slap on the wrist for serious offenses. Here are a few that resulted in suspensions at the high school level, but the parent wanted no consequence at all or something very light certainly not the suspension that was handed down.

A parent threatened to get a lawyer and sue the athletic director when his daughter was suspended from school and released from the girl's hockey team after being caught smoking outside the arena after a hockey game. He was angrier over no more hockey than the school suspension or the fact that his 16-year-old was smoking.

A boy sucker punched another boy. The parents were angry and said, "You can't suspend him because you're giving him a vacation. He'll just play and ride his four-wheeler the whole time." Of course, telling a parent how they should be parenting in a situation like this was useless.

Teachers overheard a girl threaten to slit another girl's throat, saying if she couldn't get it done at school she would go to her house and get her over the upcoming school vacation.

A girl who was pregnant was called a whore by another girl in a public setting and stated with vulgarity how many boys the girl had been with.

Another student called a teacher a douche bag.

A boy threatened that he would get his dad's gun when he got home that night and come to school the next day and shoot as many staff as he could. The parents actually stated, "He wasn't serious, it was just talking, he didn't do anything."

In another situation a student physically groped a female staff member.

Another told a teacher what a nice ass she had.

There were countless instances of students telling teachers to do something anatomically impossible. None of these warranted any consequence in the parents' eyes.

One time a mother, not signing in as required at the office, made a beeline to her child's classroom and screamed obscenities, literally inches from the teacher's face in front of the class, as well as threatening her with bodily harm. What was the crime the teacher committed? Giving the student an "F". I ended up banning the woman from the school grounds for the year and had the local sheriff's office serve her a "do not trespass" order.

I also encountered a high school student downtown with his mother when I was going to deposit funds into a school account. I asked her why he wasn't in school. "Oh, I called him in sick. He's not really sick, he's just under the weather." Really? That was the best she could do?

Here's part of an angry parent's email, a rant that went on for four pages but these quotes will make the point. "I am not interested in this teacher's motives but I am very concerned about her actions in placing an "F" on my son's report card. Depending on our proceedings in this case I may retain counsel. Her actions are negatively impacting my son's emotional, physical, and academic well-being." Apparently she felt that threat of getting an attorney would scare me into forcing a teacher to change a grade that a student earned.

There was a mom who came into the office one morning. Her daughter had refused to participate in physical education class. The girl had actually told the teacher on previous occasions that she didn't want to do anything that might make her sweat. This mom announced to the secretary, "She can't do gym today. She's been to the doctor and he says she may have a cracked hip." Mind you, the daughter had walked into the office without so much as a limp and had perfect posture. When I questioned the mom about a doctor's note her response was, "Oh, I forgot to get one." I told the mom we would need a note from the doctor to avoid a negative grade for non-participation. Of course, no note ever came.

A parent was wildly upset because we suspended her son who had tried to suffocate another student with a down-filled jacket. "He would not have done that."

I had a five-year-old using extremely vulgar language at a kindergarten teacher complete with kicking, spitting, and biting. Yet the parent was angry that her child had to be restrained, completely ignoring the child's behavior.

A mother came to the high school with the intent to physically assault someone else's child because of jealousy over her over her daughter's boyfriend.

I had a parent serve detention for her child because the child had been held accountable for not turning back in a parental signed progress report. Without that back the teacher had no way of knowing if the parent actually saw the progress report. It avoids parent complaints at report card time that they were unaware that their child was in academic trouble.

An armed man was apprehended on his way to the high school who had the intention of taking his biological child, though he no longer had custodial rights.

There was a student who was constantly in trouble and had been suspended multiple times. The parent came in to get the child and hear what had happened. I explained that she was being suspended. That day alone she had threatened to get a gun from home and shoot a staff member, physically assaulted another student, striking them in the back of the head, was caught smoking on school grounds, and after being told she was being suspended for her actions threatened that when she returned she would "bash the other student's head in with a rock."

Upon hearing this plethora of offenses, the father not only said it was "stupid" to suspend his daughter, but also said that "I made up my own rules and was running a military concentration camp." He knew I had been in the military before my education career. I told him, "No, I don't make up rules, just follow existing ones."

Of course, once again, this parent decided social media was the place to air out what "I had done to his daughter", without ever mentioning the above behaviors that got her suspended. He also stated kids should be able to swear in school because they hear it in society anyway. At that point, you know the caliber of who you are dealing with and once again you can't talk rationally with irrational people. Facts don't mitigate their view at all.

I had one dad who was taking his son out of school for a fishing trip and lied that his son had a doctor's appointment in a different town. When it was challenged and a doctor's note asked for, the dad landed in my office screaming, "I guess we have an asshole running the high school, and we need to get rid of you. How dare you challenge my integrity?"

I responded, "We can ask for a doctor's note for one thing, but the real clincher was the other guy you are going fishing with who told me about it."

I once had a parent say to me about 6 months into my tenure, "We didn't have a drug problem at this school until you showed up." Of course, what had actually happened was my aggressive action to clean up the mess.

One high school student was failing virtually every subject. She truly could not afford to miss any instruction. The parents wanted to take a three-week vacation to Florida right after the winter one-week break, even though their daughter was doing so poorly. I disapproved their request. They, of course, went anyway and then appealed to the school board when the girl couldn't make up work missed due to it being an unexcused absence. Once the board was aware of the facts, they supported me.

I once had a student who was pretending to be sick. The nurse said she had no fever and appeared fine. She was a habitual truant and was in serious trouble academically. She called her grandmother on a cell and left anyway without permission and was given appropriate consequences for skipping school. The father, after hearing about the consequences, said to me, "What kind of bullshit games are you playing here? You don't belong around kids."

Another parent said to my boss, the superintendent, that I threatened his son with a three day suspension if he didn't comply with what I had requested. I had actually kept him from being suspended by giving him a choice at redemption for what he had done because the consequence if he continued, according to our student handbook, was suspension.

A boy was suspended for having sex in school, and then calling the teacher, who caught him and his girlfriend, a fucking bitch. He told his parents that he had said "This is friggin bullshit." The parents believed their son and saw that this whole thing was not a big deal. In fact the mom, on her way out, said "I can't believe you're suspending him just for fucking."

A boy was not allowed to go to Prom as he had refused to serve detention time he owed. The parent called the superintendent to report that "I was out to get his son."

Parents saw no issue with all the following incidents:

A student who missed detention time for "a family emergency" but was seen an hour later in attendance at an away JV basketball game.

A purse searched due to reasonable suspicion of carrying drugs, which revealed condoms and tampons in the purse as well as drugs. In the parent view, she can't be accountable for the drugs due to the school embarrassingly revealing she had condoms and tampons in her purse.

From fictitious doctor appointments to deaths in the family, parents, rather than build a trusting relationship and just tell the truth and ask for help when an absence is needed, often fabricated. Some were so frequent I required a note from the doctor's office indicating an appointment. One student revealed to me her mom had stolen a ream of appointment slips from an office to use to make up excuses.

The saddest part of these several pages of stupid parent tricks is that I haven't even touched the surface. There was a 17-year-old student who rolled over his car. He had always had a bad temper and was constantly on the edge of trouble. His mother was notorious for defending even the most outrageous behavior. She continuously behaved like a bully with staff, screaming her demands be met and her son, in her view, was to never be held accountable for anything.

At the rollover accident scene, her son blew a 1.5 on the Breathalyzer and was criminally charged with an OUI. This mom showed up at the scene and began her screaming rant at the police in the same style she tried to bully staff at school. By not stopping, impeding, and threatening, the police ended up nearly arresting her, and in fact, she was detained and told she would be arrested if she continued to impede the police.

She did not get her way in keeping her son from heading to jail that night or his being charged with an OUI. Multiple staff, who had tried to work with this woman, felt Karma had interceded. As an example, this same Mom had walked past the office, did not sign in, went to a classroom and got in the face of a teacher, screaming obscenities at the teacher in front of the teacher's class over a grade her son had received. "That teacher is trying to keep my son from playing football." That was the concern, not that her son was failing a class.

Then there was the time Dad called my boss, the superintendent, outraged that "Mr. Atwood called my daughter a bitch." I'd actually told him his daughter was a *habitual* truant.

Generally speaking, after dealing with the parent or parents, you had a good idea of why their child acted the way he did. The majority of parents were rational, could see the point and worked with the school. Parental involvement is so important.

Why is there an M in our name?

At times I was astounded at how bright and talented some students were. I was equally astounded at the dimness of some student's bulb. Here are just a few examples.

An extensive renovation was taking place in my high school. As part of that, our school's name was emblazoned in school colors into the tiles on the floor at the school entrance, facing the door so that when people entered you couldn't help but notice the classy emblem.

A high school sophomore, who saw me standing in the entrance one day asked me, "Why does it have an M at the beginning of our name? Our school name starts with a W?"

I thought she was joking at first, but she was serious. I walked her around to the door and suggested she look at it again. She'd been looking at it upside down.

One girl told me she didn't attend school the previous day because her hair hurt.

A young driver asked me for a handicapped parking sticker directly in front of the school because his arm was in a cast, so he couldn't walk from the student parking area.

A student accused me of giving him a detention because he was Polish.

One girl skipped an after school detention which resulted in a three hour Friday night detention. Then she skipped that too, and got a five day suspension with a requirement to serve the three hour detention before being allowed to return to school. She said she shouldn't be held accountable because her meds made her do it, an excuse her parents supported. I requested a Doctor's note, which of course was never produced so the consequences stood.

A boy, whose parents also supported his view, said that he should be allowed to say shit in school as it is not swearing.

One girl, who had two children before she entered her junior year, asked for an excused absence from school to get a pregnancy test kit. "We want a third child."

A boy vehemently denied cheating even though answers were written all over his arms under his long sleeve shirt.

Another student refused to pay for textbooks he had been seen stuffing into a toilet. "Those books are crap so that's where they belong."

As I've already related, there were multiple occasions of angry parents saying their child was being bullied, but since the student hadn't reported it we couldn't investigate. Said one boy: "I should know what happened in my school." Parents often supported this view, that in a school of 600 students, I should magically know about an incident that happened in a student bathroom that was never reported.

A girl went home and told her parents the school was offering a class called "History of Farts." Of course I got a call demanding to know what kind of school was I running here?! The class was "A History of Art."

A kid stole a cheeseburger from the lunch line by hiding it in his armpit.

One student was suspended for bringing alcohol in an orange juice bottle; she was drinking screwdrivers. Her parents hired a lawyer to try and sue the school because of the "emotional trauma" of being suspended, which led to grades going down because she had been traumatized by the suspension.

A boy announced at an assembly before a performance on the piano that he would be "playing with himself."

A parent supported their son's almost daily lateness, saying that he was tired and should be allowed to come in late; he needs his sleep.

Another student broke the glass on a copier because he sat on it and tried to copy his rear end.

"Pat" from Saturday Night Live

Remember how several of the *Saturday Night Live* actors diligently, week after week, tried to figure out the gender of "Pat", the character in a regular skit who had relatively short curly black hair and who dressed in jeans and a plaid shirt? Each week the cast asked probing questions, trying to figure out if he/she was male or female. This story reminds me of those wildly popular skits.

The principal was unfamiliar with the school's version of Pat, a girl whose dress and mannerisms were very much like a boy. Her voice was the give-away.

He thought she was a "he", and when he saw her headed into the girls bathroom he yelled at the top of his lungs, "Hey, where do you think you are going!?!!"

Pat ignored him and went into the bathroom. The principal got to her as she was about to turn the corner into the bathroom and grabbed her by the arm.

"I asked you where you thought you were going."

Pat, which of course is not her real name, said very matter of factly, "Because I'm a girl and I have to pee, is that ok?"

Deer in the headlight look does not even begin to describe the utter shock on the principal's face. He was so sure this was a boy and so shocked that he was wrong that all he could eke out was a muffled, "ah, ok."

I'd only been at that high school for a month as the assistant principal. I still remember the look on his face; it was classic. You had to be there to fully appreciate how funny it was, but trust me, to this day it still makes me smile.

Would Not Have Happened

Al, a high school sophomore was failing miserably with just one credit that he had earned his freshman year. Though he was a capable student, he came from a poor home environment and simply did not care about his education. He exerted absolutely no effort and likely would not breathe if it wasn't involuntary.

However, there was a special education teacher who simply would not give up on him. She tried so hard with him over and over again. She knew he could do it, but raw ability never wrote a good paper. One has to actually do the work to show.

The teacher had handled Al with kid gloves throughout the quarter, but was becoming very frustrated at his lack of engagement. So she changed tactics and began hounding him constantly. Al would sometimes give in and show a little effort, mostly I think to get this teacher off his back.

Then, one day, he was having none of it. No matter how many times she provided support materials or offered advice, he just refused to engage. She got more and more direct until about the fifth or sixth time she asked why he hadn't started the work, he'd had enough.

"Why don't you just blow me?" he said loud enough for all the students in the room to hear, naturally resulting in some laughter.

Insulted and incensed doesn't begin to describe how this teacher felt. Al, was sent to my office where he didn't deny what he had said. In fact he called her a bitch during his conversation with me. I never shared that with the teacher. I suspended him for his utter disrespect to the teacher and the disruption it caused to the class.

At the end of the day, the teacher bee-lined to my office to see what I'd done. She was satisfied at the way I'd handled it. After a brief conversation about how to work with Al on his return, she said "I just couldn't believe he would tell me to blow him!"

Then, saying, as she turned to leave the office and without missing a beat "Besides, I would never have considered it."

Free Turkey at Thanksgiving

Educators deal with long hours and tough issues with many aspects of their students'
lives. If you are nothing but serious all the time and have
no sense of humor then the tough stuff will eat you up.

Two teachers pulled a prank that backfired on
them. One morning during the lead up to the short break
for Thanksgiving they were both in the teacher's lounge
during their planning periods. The school librarian came
in to grab her lunch in the fridge.

The social studies teacher asked her, "Have you
gotten your free turkey yet?"

"What turkey?"

"The turkey Mr. Atwood is giving to all staff as an
appreciation for our work here."

"No."

The P.E. teacher chimed in: "You'd better get
down there because the turkeys were running low, and
there may not be enough for everyone."

She took them at their word and headed to my office.

Of course, those two were no doubt laughing at
the set up, and how embarrassed she'd be when she
asked me for her turkey.

The puzzled look on my face when she said she'd
come for her turkey immediately gave away that she had
been bamboozled.

She turned red and apologized, telling me about
the two culprits in the teachers' room, two fellows I
knew were perfectly capable of such a prank. I told her to
not say a word to them and to come back to my office in

30 minutes. I knew the manager of the local supermarket and gave him a call.

He happened to have a great sale going on with turkeys. I went down to the store, which was nearby, and grabbed a small, 10 pound bird. I came back, gave the librarian the bird, and told her to go to each of the teachers' classrooms, open their door briefly, hold up the turkey and thank them for the tip; they were right, yes indeed, there were only a few turkeys left.

Both of these teachers showed up at my office directly after the dismissal bell, asking me about a turkey. I acted shocked and asked them what on earth they were talking about? I still remember the look of disbelief on their faces that the mild mannered librarian had turned the tables on them.

One footnote to this story. The store manager the next day let me buy a bunch of eight to ten pound birds at $.39 cents a pound. It was a great idea and I did in fact end up giving my very hard working staff turkeys for Thanksgiving.

The Wastebasket

Teenage pranks are usually harmless and cause no real problem, but this one infuriated a teacher. This guy apparently had no sense of humor whatsoever, and I must say it privately gave me a chuckle.

Whenever Mr. Jones' wastebasket started looking full, he would stomp it down violently, almost as though he was angry at the thing. This aggressiveness was well known to his students.

But one day when he pounced and attacked it, he did not get the expected result. Somebody had filled it part way with water, covered that with a sheet of plastic, and then meticulously layered trash over the top of that.

The first aggressive stomp soaked the teacher's pants to the crotch so that it looked like he had wet himself. He was absolutely furious, and when the class erupted in laughter, he demanded to know who the perpetrator was.

When everyone denied it he threatened the entire class with a consequence if they didn't divulge the perpetrator.

Finally he called me to his room. I had to take him out into the hall and remind him that he had taught several periods that day; it could have been a student from any class. I never did find out who pulled that prank. Mr. Jones no longer stomped down his trash.

Don't Eat It

I learned pretty early on that it may not be a great idea to eat something that high school students had prepared for you. It could be an opportunity to seek revenge for a well-deserved consequence.

But one teacher would give students money to pick up lunch for him in the school cafeteria. He paid the staff rate for his lunch which was more than students paid; he wasn't trying to get his lunch cheaper, he just didn't want to walk to the cafeteria.

So one day, shortly after having his chef salad, he started vomiting. He said he had been feeling fine up to lunch so he figured his lunch didn't agree with him, perhaps something was spoiled on his salad. Maybe, he said, I should check that out with the cafeteria so that no one else would get sick.

He went home, and I got an ed tech to cover his classes the remaining two hours of the day. I checked with the cafeteria, but there didn't seem to be a problem with spoiled food.

After school, a student asked to speak to me confidentially. I told her I couldn't guarantee she would not be in trouble if she'd done something wrong. She said she hadn't, but felt too guilty and so bothered by what had happened to the teacher that she had to tell me.

The students who got the teacher's lunch had mixed some Ipecac syrup (used to induce vomiting) in with the salad dressing. The teacher learned a tough lesson, and I held the perpetrators accountable. And of course, the parents fought me on my actions, but to no avail.

I am not Skipping School

A rumor went around that a certain Friday in June was going to be "senior skip day." I got wind of this and warned students that they could jeopardize going on the senior trip or other consequences for skipping school *en masse*.

It worked and most did not skip school that day. One girl, a very good student, well rounded and usually very reliable, called me at the office on the so-called skip day. She had just heard about skip day, and was (legitimately) at the doctor's office when she found out.

She'd called to give this long explanation about scheduling it before she realized it was skip day, and that she would be bringing me in a doctor's note, and she'd be back by lunch time, etc.

There was no doubt in my mind that it was legit; this girl was a joy to be around. But she ended the conversation with a habit many have adopted with family members; "Ok then, see you soon, love you, I MEAN, I MEAN, bye" and then just hung up in embarrassment.

She avoided me during the few remaining days till graduation, not even looking in my direction. At graduation night, with close to two thousand family and friends in attendance, I read each student's name as they crossed the stage, shook hands and handed them their diploma. With a couple of thousand people applauding, no one could hear me.

When her turn came I said, "Amanda, I love you too." Nobody knew why she was so red-faced as she walked off the stage. She is closing in on 40 now, and I wonder if she has ever told anyone how she told her principal she loved him.

The Doctor's Note

Sometimes students (and their enabling parents) used legitimate doctor's notes in ways they weren't intended. One student complained that he wanted a top locker versus the bottom locker he'd been assigned. Locker assignments were just the luck of the draw. Of course everyone wanted a top locker; you don't have to bend down, and it's more convenient.

"You'll be hearing from my mother," the boy said when I told him I wouldn't change his locker. I had dealt with his mother before, and she was not only a helicopter parent, but also would do anything he wanted.

Mom came in saying because her son was tall he had to have an upper locker. When I explained about locker assignments, she became angry and said she'd be back. The next day she came back with not one, but three doctor's notes on the doctor's letterhead;

The first: "Due to his height, Johnny should be given a top locker. He is 6'4" and he has difficulty bending down and from a medical standpoint should not be doing so."

The second: "Johnny should be permitted to carry his backpack through the school." We had a rule that backpacks couldn't be carried through the school day for a couple reasons. No student needed books for more than two classes without an opportunity to revisit the locker. Backpacks are bulky and take up so much room between rows of desks that they're a tripping hazard. Plus, contraband could be concealed and carried in backpacks.

I tried to contact the doctor, but he cited patient privacy and wouldn't speak with me. I don't know why he'd written this, but I was firm; I simply said no. Mom did not agree, but dropped that one. However, she was adamant about the top locker, especially since a doctor said it was medically necessary that her son not bend down.

But since her son was a hockey player, and just by the nature of that game bending over constantly handling the stick and puck, I immediately suspended him from the hockey team.

Of course mom landed in my office within an hour or so demanding he be re-instated on the team. I pulled out the very note she had produced. "Your doctor says right here in writing that medically your son should not be bending down at all. He constantly does so playing hockey so therefore for his own safety, he won't be playing hockey."

"You can't do that!"

"Actually, yes I can. Athletics are a privilege, not a right. They are not part of your son's free and appropriate education, and if your doctor says he should not be bending down, then we are not taking that chance with hockey."

The look on her face was priceless. She was not getting her way with evidence that she herself had produced for me. She left in a huff, and I thought that was the end of the story. Two days later her son brought me another note from the same doctor that read, "Johnny is healthy and able to play hockey." I told the boy that the two doctor's notes were in direct conflict with each other and until I spoke to the doctor to clear it up he would not be playing hockey.

Magically, the doctor who earlier wouldn't discuss a patient's case with me called within the hour. He confidently told me what a pain this mom was, and it was just easier to do what she wanted. I went over both notes, and he agreed they were in conflict.

He faxed me a clarifying note indicating bending over was no problem at all. The student agreed to comply with his initial locker assignment if he could go back on the hockey team. I didn't hear from the mom, but I was told she skewered me all over Facebook, complete with false information.

I should mention the third note that was about her daughter. "Suzy, due to her height, (5'9"), medically needs to be given an upper locker rather than a lower one as she should not be bending down." The daughter, who was also into co-curricular activities, did not balk at the locker assignment after the issue with her brother played out.

Another mother came in to my office just wild about her son's placement in a certain academic class. She did not like the caliber of some students in that class. During the conversation I said, "We always try to place students in heterogeneous groups." The mom then became very angry insisting that "my son is not heterogeneous, he has always liked girls!!"

Then there was the parent who wanted me to write a letter to get a good student discount on his car insurance. Although the boy's grades were decent, he had been suspended for carrying a knife in school, caught with cigarettes and with rolling papers. When I reminded the father of all this he said, "Well he's over 18 so it's legal for him to smoke and carry a knife."

The growing drug problem had not been addressed at one high school where I worked. When I tackled it head on with suspensions, and in the case of dealers, a couple of expulsions, our statistics and incidents steadily diminished. Within just three years those stats were ten percent of what they were when I initially arrived. A parent with a son who'd been suspended for marijuana possession was aware that the problems that first year had been addressed. Her last comment to me as she angrily left with her suspended son was "We didn't have a drug problem here at this school until you showed up."

Teenage Raging Hormones

Every student was issued a laptop at the beginning of the year. They could take them home and many professed how academics would surely improve. In my experience, grades actually went down in many cases, not to mention all the problems that were created.

For example, even though the school's server had a decent filter to blocked sites, once student accessed outside servers they could go anywhere on line, and did. Because it is so easy to say something to a computer that you wouldn't say to someone's face, bullying, threatening, and sexual harassment issues skyrocketed. Additionally, posting of inappropriate photos of themselves along with Skyping live sexual acts also added to the fun of dealing with these issues.

One young man masturbated for his girlfriend on Skype and in return she did the same with a blue hair brush. It almost became a game with some students; who could be the most out there. We had some very upset parents when we investigated these cases, and refused to let students take their computers home. Not only were kids losing out on a valuable educational tool, but that the parent could no longer use it, and as wrong as this sounds, it was sometimes the parents going to inappropriate sites.

The health teacher, when she got to the unit on sexuality, put out a box for questions about sex that students were afraid to ask. Here are some she fielded:

Can I get pregnant having anal sex?

Why does my erect penis always lean to the left?

Can I get pregnant performing oral sex?

I often throw up when I have sex with my boy-friend so can I be allergic to having sex with him?

What size condoms should I buy if I am average size?

The ignorance of the subject was quite alarming, as was the pretty outlandish behavior brought on by their teenage hormones. There was an ongoing problem at one school with "oral sex races." In December and January, when days are the shortest, a majority of the ride to school happens in the dark, particularly in areas where the trip to school begins early with an hour long bus ride. Couple that with the decision by some districts to save money by having a single bus run for all students K-12 riding the same bus instead of having an elementary and a secondary run.

From younger children being bullied to students having sex on the buses, I dealt with many problems. A first grade parent landed in my office, wanting my head on a platter. It always amazed me that many parents blew up at school administrators over things that either the school was unaware of, which was the case here, or had no control over. Yet somehow, I was to be blamed.

Her child had come home from school and de-scribed in extreme graphic detail the oral sex contest that she had witnessed on the bus. I assured her this would be fully investigated, and action taken, and of course I would have put a stop to this had I known about it.

Upon investigation, it turned out to not only be true, but had been going on for a while. One girl readily admitted and told all because she was angry that her boyfriend had participated in the "race" even though she had not been on the bus. She was mad at the girl who had been involved with the boyfriend, but not at him, which defies logic as far as I am concerned.

After students had been disciplined with school and bus suspensions, drivers were told to be sure students were segregated on the buses in three groups of elementary, middle, and high school with serious consequences for violators. This had always been the rule but on that dark ride, it had not been enforced very well.

Outrageous Behavior

I sometimes shared a few stories, minus names of course, at a local hangout in my hometown. I distinctly remember the following conversation with a friend :

"All that crap happened at your school this year?"

"All that happened today."

A sophomore encouraging a fifth grader to commit suicide.

A girl wearing a t-shirt that read, "Rub here for luck."

Lots and lots of incidents with tobacco and marijuana.

Lots of forged bus notes.

Lots of threatening, fights, assaults, bullying, etc.

Lots of teachers told by lots of students to "go f-themselves.

A student told a bus driver to "shut up bitch and just drive the bus."

A girl with a penis-shaped lollipop, given to her by her mom.

A snowman in front of the school complete with a carrot penis and two oranges for testicles.

A couple of students caught having a physical interlude in the girls bathroom stall, the boy standing on the toilet and his girlfriend straddling him so no feet could be seen in the stall. Once caught the boy told me "Whatever I get for this, it was so worth it."

One boy asked me to suspend him because if I didn't he would strangle another student to death.

Extremely detailed pornographic art on bathroom walls.

A student we dubbed "the mad crapper" because he'd urinate and defecate on the floor next to the toilet and in the sink.

"This is his purse," taped to a male teachers backpack.

"I ain't fucking doing that," addressed to a teacher.

A bus-full of students mooning a line of cars on the highway.

Inappropriate language, e.g. *faggot*, condoned by some parents.

Hell hath no fury like a scorned high school girl. Hair pulling, knock down, fist fights, spray painting a rival's car, smashing out said rival's car windows, harboring resentment from literally years earlier, calling above-mentioned rival "a nasty bitch I bet she has bugs in her c__."

Boys were no slouch in this department. Punching and fracturing the jaw of the boy another one suspected of sleeping with his girlfriend.

When we had strong evidence that a girl was doing drugs and that her boyfriend was her supplier, we searched his backpack. Not only did we find drugs but it wasn't pleasant to find a used condom.

One teacher, a very mild mannered fellow, was too much of a softie. Things were out of hand by the time he reported to me that some boys were verbally assaulting him; his classroom was out of control. Of course, the students vehemently denied the behavior, disrespect, foul language, throwing things, and much more.

He had a storage closet in the room with one-way glass in the door. One day I hid in that closet to observe the class; some six boys were involved and their behavior was outrageous. The look on their faces when their principal opened that door was memorable to say the least. They knew I had witnessed it all, and even then some tried to deny to no avail.

A girl flashed a tampon at a teacher when asked to see her hall pass, saying "if I don't get to the bathroom soon to use this there is going to be an awful mess."

I had confiscated a student cell phone just before going into a meeting because he was using it in his class. Five minutes later the phone rang. A kid on the other end says, "Hey." I respond "Hey, how you doing?" The kid goes on about meeting after school at a certain location to "finish up the deal."

"Why are you calling Johnny while he is in school?"

"Who is this?"

"His principal." There was a long moment of silence. "I took his cell phone because he was using it during class time. If he does it again he won't get it back, and his parents will have to come get it. Do him a favor and don't call him again during school hours and risk him losing it, ok?"

"Uh...ok."

"Have a good day, bye, bye."

A girl, who'd come to us from Kansas, wore a t-shirt that read "Not Everything in Kansas is Flat."

A boy's shirt read "All Bad Girls Report To My Room."

Another said, "Do you believe in love at first sight or do I need to walk by you again?"

The health class was studying the harmful effects of steroid use. One student said he'd read it could cause impotence and hardening of the clitoris. "What's a clitoris?" he asked.

The boy thought his classmates were giggling because he ought to know, so he quickly said, "Oh, never mind, I know; it's that yellow book over on the shelf" pointing to the thesaurus.

"Miss Smith," a boy asked, "when you erase the board would you please do it side to side and not up and down?"

"Why?"

"Because then your backside won't wiggle so much."

The athletic director asked me to look at video tape from the athletic field camera. We'd installed it after cars had been driven on the field and torn it up. Instead we'd caught a high school couple having oral sex in the dugout. It certainly was tough starting that conversation with parents.

I stopped a couple who were both coming out of the boys' bathroom. "Why were you both in there?" When I got no answer, that was the answer.

"I know you can't smoke on school grounds," one boy told me, "so can I sign out of my study hall and go a couple streets over to have a cigarette?"

Like many teenage girls Amy, a recent graduate who'd been a pretty good student, was attracted to bad boys. She emailed me: "Dear Mr. Atwood, I am still working at Mister Market and I am a bagger. I really miss John Smith so much. Do you know what county jail or state jail he went to?"

Here's a letter a girl received from a former student: "If you don't accept this policy, then don't sign it and work for me. If you're reading this then I have offered you a spot, in the porno movies I make. You must have a photo ID, and I will make a copy of this. Must be at least 18 years of age to be in these movies. The pay will go if I make money selling the movies, then you will get money. If I can't sell them then you can sue me for not paying you. So don't expect to get paid till they sell. If you sign this then I expect you to do your job, the way I want it done."

After involving the police I didn't hear any more about it, and the former student never surfaced on school grounds again.

I had a parent come with clean shoes and socks for her five-year-old who'd urinated in them, and then put them back on.

Two high schoolers left campus, broke into a church, and vandalized the expensive organ after drinking themselves into a stupor.

A student who was not allowed to bring his car to school after multiple violations took his parents' car with their permission, thinking he'd wouldn't get caught. This may have worked if he hadn't parked their car in a handicapped parking spot and got towed.

One boy who considered himself a body-builder wondered if taking steroids would make his large penis smaller.

Another boy left class on a bathroom pass and hopped onto the vocational school bus. We initially thought he'd skipped school until he was caught wandering around the vocational center. Thinking he was from one of the outlying towns that served the voc school I asked, "where are you from, Allan?"

He responded, "Connecticut."

And then there was the boy who decided to lay down in front of a school bus in protest. Of course, he didn't realize that being that close to the front of the bus the driver couldn't see him. Luckily the bus went over him without hitting him. When he screamed, the driver stopped –he was a couple of feet under the bus.

When I spoke with a girl about her revealing top she said, "I can't help it that I am so well-endowed that they don't make a shirt that can cover me up."

One student enrolled after the school year had started. Thirty minutes into his first day he was led away by police in handcuffs, and I don't even know why. I never saw him again.

A boy was sent home wearing a t-shirt that read "I love the four B's: Breasts, Butts, Bellies and Bras".

His dad said "I didn't send him back to school after you sent him home to change because it doesn't matter anyway. I skipped at least one class a week when I was in high school, and it didn't hurt me any." Of course, he didn't work, and the family lived in a 30-year-old broken down, single-wide trailer.

Parents and/or students could opt out of the Psychology class unit on Human Sexuality. Before starting the unit the teacher said, "If the content makes you uncomfortable you can go next door for an alternative educational activity."

One student asked, "Is it an alternative sexual activity?"

A boy had a behavior contract that included his writing a letter of apology to a staff member and having his parent sign it. It was due on Monday.

Monday he "forgot."

Tuesday "he didn't get around to it yet." I warned him of further consequences if it didn't get in on Wednesday.

On Wednesday he said his mother refused to sign it and gave me both her work and home phone number. When I called the mother she told me pull it out of her son's ass as he was too stupid to put in in his pocket as she had asked him to.

Like most schools, we had a marquee out in front with a sign telling of current events and happenings at the school. One morning I found the sign had been altered. The sign put up the day before read "Good Luck Girls." We wish you well in Saturday's state championship game." Someone had broken into the sign and with black marker changed the L in Luck to an F.

A boy said to a young teacher, "Ms. Smith, you have a really nice ass." She told me later, "I didn't know how to respond. Should I have said thank you?"

An out-of-control student took a swing at a teacher, trying to punch him in the face. The teacher bending backwards barely evaded the punch. Several other teachers stepped in, but before they could restrain him the student turned and smashed his head into a plate glass window, shattering the window.

Teacher Stupid Tricks

Teachers are human and most are very professional. However, I had a few teachers work for me over my 22 years and five schools that left me wondering about what could they have been thinking? A few of these had to be fired, and it will likely be obvious which of these stories may have led to that. Most of these though are just bonehead moves that will beg that same question. What the heck were they thinking?

There was the teacher who said to a boy who was recovering from mono that "I'd like you to come kiss me so I can go out on sick leave." She thought it was funny. The parent didn't think so.

A teacher allowed a parent to take posed pictures of other people's children in her classroom and then post them on social media.

Then there were the times I specifically asked that a student be sent to me, and then the teacher never told the kid. I ended up chasing him from class to class. When I nailed him for avoiding me he'd say "But Mr. Atwood, she never told me."

I was called to a hallway to deal with a fistfight between two boys. These two boys had originally been fighting in a classroom, and the teacher's solution was to send the two of them to the office at the same time, completely unsupervised and without notifying anyone that they were coming. What would you expect to happen with two unsupervised boys going to the office when they had just been pulled apart?

A teacher was quite literally falling down drunk in his classroom. He was so wasted that he couldn't, on his own, negotiate the door to get out of the classroom or negotiate the door leading into my office without bumping into the door frame. When the SRO finally got hold of a Breathalyzer, the teacher blew a blood alcohol content 2.5 times the legal limit for intoxication. The union tried to say the teacher's meds didn't allow his liver to process the alcohol he had consumed the night before. It was ludicrous. The teacher resigned a couple of months later when it became obvious he was about to be fired.

A 22-year-old long term substitute teacher was sleeping with one of his 17-year-old students.

Another teacher, who was also a basketball coach, was sleeping with his 17-year-old team manager. He was so brazen that it astounded me. The girl's parents would go to the freshman game to watch the girl's younger brother play. Knowing the parents were at the school the teacher/coach would go to her house and sleep with the girl, while the parents were at the brother's game. The two would come back to the school for the JV game, and then he would coach the varsity game in front of the parents. They got caught because of the texting going back and forth on the girl's cell phone. From some of the correspondence, you would swear these were two 16-year-olds in mad puppy love.

An athletic director who left the mike on at a basketball game and made a comment about one of our team's players, saying, "He's being real pissy with the official and he's going to end up getting a "T". The parents were not pleased.

Parent teacher conferences were held in the fall and in the spring. Conferences lasted until 8, making it a 15-hour day for teachers. As I walked down the hall to check that people were wrapping it up I spotted the principal and the school nurse sitting side by side on a bench.

Both of them were obviously tired. The nurse, after yawning as I went by, pointed back and forth between herself and the principal, saying "We're going to be in bed by 9 tonight." The principal, seeing the look on my face added, "Yes, but with other people."

One teacher union rep wasn't the sharpest knife in the drawer. After a rather heated discussion about the behavior of a certain teacher, he had a much different view after learning the facts. The teacher had kept him in the dark up to that point, leaving him with a little egg on his face.

When things were wrapped up, he said "Well, hindsight is always 50-50." After a long rather challenging day it gave everyone in the room a chuckle after he left the room, particularly because he said it with such an air of seriousness.

A school nurse unfortunately had breast cancer and had to undergo a double mastectomy. When she returned to work after this life threatening medical issue she came in my office on her first day back and said, "Look at these. Of course they're fake, but they look alright don't they?"

I didn't respond at first and just managed a muffled "ya." I was a little uncomfortable, but it didn't seem to bother her any.

A teacher was discussing Y and X chromosomes and examples of male and female configurations. When a student asked how to tell the difference in a sample, the teacher said, "If you want to see if it is a male or female just pull down their genes."

When an attractive, young teacher came into the teacher's room wearing a new fur coat another teacher mentioned that it was a nice looking coat. Her response:

"Do you want to touch my fur?" which caused milk to come out of a colleagues nose, he laughed so hard.

When the school nurse showed me the document she'd prepared on a student I couldn't believe she'd written in several places that the student would "F - up". She informed me that was a common abbreviation on medical documents for *follow up.*

A teacher told high school students that she really liked getting her hair done at Studio 69 because it was so personal there. Of course, snickering greeted that. Teenagers can twist anything.

For example, a science teacher was discussing friction and said, "One way to eliminate friction is to use lubrication." That's all it took to get a few students giggling.

The French teacher who did a fun little activity where she had students pretending to be an animal and say in French what color they were, their size, what they liked to eat, etc., until the rest of the students could accurately guess what animal they were. It went well until the end when the teacher said, "Next week, you will all have to be a vegetable and I will participate as well. I'm going to be a desirable vegetable, but I'm not going to let anybody eat me."

The teacher who was explaining about interviewing skills: "At some point," he said, " you'll all have to sell yourselves to somebody." That's all it took. He lost them for ten minutes

The elementary school secretary checked winter morning temps to be sure it was warm enough to have outside recess. She was doing this from her home computer before leaving for work. Her email response was this, "Yes, I do it at home and I also have the vibration machine." I have no idea what she was talking about.

The school nurse came to me in a panic because she had tried to call the poison control number using the school phone. She was one number off and got an inappropriate location by dialing 1-900 instead of 1-800. She was very embarrassed and wanted me to know what had happened as she didn't want anyone thinking she was calling those type of numbers on a school phone.

Another staff member doing research for a class project tried to do an internet search on the White House in Washington D.C. However, she got a porn site. Apparently *white house dot org* or *dot net* or whatever she typed, linked to a porn site. Once there, every time she tried to get out of it, it would link to something else. She too was over the moon embarrassed and did not want the impression out there that she was searching those sites with a school laptop. The kids were in hysterics and the teacher was worried that some of the kids would undoubtedly tell their parents.

A teacher who, though she was quick to point out inappropriate behavior to me, did not address it herself. For instance, she walked around the gymnasium to report to me that a boy was wearing a hat in school. When I pointed out that she could have told him herself, she responded, "Is it my job to do that?"

"Why yes, yes it is."

"Gary," one teacher said to another out in the hallway in earshot of several teenagers, "can you come into my room and get into my drawers?" Her drawers in her desk were sticking in the humid weather.

And this: "Robbie, did you get it up over the weekend?" Rob had a private pilot's license and had been tinkering on his small, old plane for weeks.

Referring to the collegiate scholarship offer a student had received the teacher said to a group of kids, "Johnny's got a real nice package."

And to a home economics cookie class, "Ok boys, I want you to go over there and crush your nuts on the counter."

The Knife Company

Schools are prime targets for companies looking to market items. Take "Myron" out of New Jersey. I'd received a letter from this company that included a sample of the knife they wanted our school to sell.

"We've engraved Hodgdon High School on this seven function sure grip knife so that you can see how impressive it is! Handing out custom engraved pocket knives of such quality is like putting your business card in your customers' hands every day. That's how effective the seven function sure grip knife is at building an image with prospects, maintaining goodwill and earning recognition.

"If you place your order today, I'll offer you one low price of just $1.99 per pocket knife for any quantity shown!"

This was not ancient history. The letter was dated September 2003.

Yeah, that would be a good idea, hand out knives at a public high school. It was at this point in my career that very little surprised me anymore.

Afterword

Corporate friends of mine who are college educated, working, successful professionals have asked me in the past why I went to work in public education as a second career after the military.

"After all, one of your graduate degrees is a Masters in Business, couldn't you find anything better than that?"

First of all, there needs to be a societal shift in how that profession is viewed. My friend's comment says a great deal about the current view. Every single professional, be it a doctor, lawyer, plumber, carpenter, accountant, you name it, had their start with a basic education. If one can't read for example, your chances of a rewarding and successful career are slim, both financially and intrinsically.

Educators handle two things nearest and dearest to peoples' hearts: their children and their tax money. Strong school building leadership in enabling teachers to do their jobs well is critical. The lack of respect, which continues to diminish, for these professionals devastates retention. One out of three who enter education leave it in the first three years.

Even as a teacher, it was never an 8 to 2:30 job with summers off. With three or four preps, night events, grading papers after dinner, recertification course work and professional development during the summer, it was a draining and challenging job.

As an administrator it was often an extremely intense and stress-filled 55 to 70 hour work-week. That it is demanding work understates the weighty responsibilities of the position. The ocean of paperwork has to be done nights and weekends as there's never time during the school day between meetings, staff supervision and always, in high school especially, the volatile interruptions.

That all said, this profession truly does make a difference. For example, you may have a student who seemingly doesn't stand a chance of becoming a successful, contributing member of society. That student may have a father in prison and a drug-addicted mother. The student doesn't know where his next meal will come from or if the current boyfriend will beat him tonight while mom is drugged out. It is pretty hard to care about math homework in that situation.

But if an educator – teacher, principal, coach, etc. – makes a connection with that student, the one constant in his life whom he can count on who cares about his success, who holds him accountable and responsible, his trajectory can change. That is some powerful stuff.

As both a teacher and an administrator, I have had adults, former students, tell me the things I did that turned the corner for them both academically and socially. That is a feeling, I must tell you, you won't get installing a part on an assembly line making great union wages or in a corporate board meeting.

However, we need to compensate people enough to make the stress of the job worth it. In my view, money is only a motivator until you have enough. Motivation to excel goes beyond money, but you have to have enough. What we pay starting educators is pathetic. How shameful that a teacher with a spouse and two children qualifies for food stamps! These are the people who build the basic foundation of a successful society, and unless we as a society value them more than we currently do, the chance of our children getting quality people to teach them continues to decline.

Made in the USA
Middletown, DE
19 December 2019

81367920R00080